WOMEN IN CONGRESS, 1917–1990

WOMEN IN CONGRESS, 1917–1990

Prepared under the direction of the
Commission on the Bicentenary of the
U.S. House of Representatives

by the

Office of the Historian,

U.S. House of Representatives

U.S. Government Printing Office, Washington, D.C. 1991

Commission on the Bicentenary of the
U.S. House of Representatives

Lindy (Mrs. Hale) Boggs, Chairman

Members

Philip R. Sharp
Thomas M. Foglietta

Bud Shuster
Newt Gingrich
Paul B. Henry

Former Members Serving on Commission

Tom Vandergriff
John J. Rhodes

Ex-Officio Members

Richard A. Gephardt, *Majority Leader*
Robert H. Michel, *Minority Leader*

House Concurrent Resolution 167

One Hundred First Congress, First Session

Submitted by Mrs. Boggs

Resolved by the House of Representatives (the Senate concurring), That the book entitled "Women in Congress" (prepared by the Office for the Bicentennial of the House of Representatives) shall be printed as a House Document, with illustrations and suitable binding. In addition to the usual number, 25,000 copies of the book shall be printed for the use of the Office for the Bicentennial of the House of Representatives.

Approved by the House October 23, 1989.
Approved by the Senate November 20, 1989.

House Document No. 101-238, 101/2

INTRODUCTION

Since 1917 when Jeannette Rankin became the first woman to serve in the House of Representatives, 129 women have been elected or appointed to Congress. The story of their lives illustrates an important dimension of the struggle for full participation by all citizens in the political process of our national government. Their congressional service was a prominent legacy of the long campaign for woman's suffrage and for the acceptance of women in political institutions so long the exclusive domain of men. The women who have served in the House of Representatives and the Senate emerged from a wide variety of backgrounds and represented the full spectrum of American political life. Although most have supported some form of women's rights, what unites their careers is not a uniform political stance but rather a common experience with the movement to open political office to women and offer them an equal voice in the federal government.

The Commission on the Bicentenary of the U.S. House of Representatives is pleased to present this book as part of the publication program commemorating the two-hundred-year history of Congress. Included here are biographical essays on the lives of the 115 representatives and sixteen senators, including two who were previously Members of the House, who have served from forty states. In this bicentennial Congress it is appropriate to recall the advancement of women in this institution over the past seven decades. This volume was prepared by the staff of the Office of the Historian of the U.S. House of Representatives under the direction of the Commission.

Lindy (Mrs. Hale) Boggs

Lindy (Mrs. Hale) Boggs
Chairman

HAZEL HEMPEL ABEL

United States Senator
Republican of Nebraska
Eighty-third Congress
November 8, 1954–December 31, 1954

Hazel Abel was elected to the Senate to fill a two-month term left vacant by a technicality in Nebraska's election law. Eva Bowring, who was appointed to fill the vacancy in the Third District left by the death of Dwight Griswold, was barred by law from serving past the date of the first general election following her appointment. A special election open only to candidates not seeking the six-year term in the Senate, was held in November 1954. Abel, an active member of the Nebraska State Republican Party and recently-selected vice chair of the State Republican Central Committee, entered a primary crowded with fifteen other Republicans and three Democrats. She won the August primary and defeated her Democratic opponent in November. She served until December 31, 1954, when she resigned in order to give Senator-elect Carl Curtis an edge in seniority.

Abel was born Hazel Pearl Hempel in Plattsmouth, Nebraska, on July 10, 1888. She attended school in Omaha and graduated from the University of Nebraska in 1908 with a B.A. and a teacher's certificate. She taught school prior to her marriage to George Abel in 1916. Hazel Abel worked for her husband's construction firm for twenty years, and following his death in 1936 she served as company president until 1951.

During her short tenure in the Senate, Abel was appointed to the Committee on Finance and the Committee on Interstate and Foreign Commerce where she was a strong supporter of President Eisenhower. Early in her term she joined the majority in voting to censure Senator Joseph McCarthy.

Abel remained active in Republican state politics, serving as chair of the state delegation at the national convention in 1956. In 1960 she came in second place in the Republican primary for nomination as governor. Hazel Abel died in Lincoln, Nebraska, on July 30, 1966.

BELLA SAVITZKY ABZUG

United States Representative
Democrat of New York
Ninety-second–Ninety-fourth Congresses
January 3, 1971–January 3, 1977

Bella Abzug, one of the best-known Members of Congress in the 1970s, personified a widespread dissatisfaction with the traditional structure of American politics. In her first term in the House of Representatives, she challenged the seniority system and the method of committee assignment while seeking to influence the most important issues of public policy. Her congressional career followed a lifetime of civil-rights work and advo-

cacy for those she believed were unfairly excluded from the political process. Abzug's outspoken opinions and brash personal style often engendered as many opponents as supporters but always guaranteed an audience for her remarks.

Bella Savitzky was born in the Bronx on July 24, 1920, and attended public schools in New York City. As an undergraduate at

Hunter College she served as president of the student council and worked in support of the Zionist cause. During the Second World War she interrupted her law studies at Columbia University to work in a shipyard but returned to law school and was an editor of the Columbia law review before receiving her LL.B. in 1945. After entering practice, Abzug specialized in labor law but also took on a number of civil rights cases and defended individuals accused of subversive activity during the McCarthy era. In one of her most famous cases, Abzug went to Mississippi to defend Willie McGee, a black man sentenced to death after his conviction on charges of raping a white woman. In New York Abzug offered counsel to tenants' rights organizations. She was a founder and national legislative representative for the Women Strike for Peace in the 1960s. Her political activity included campaigning for Eugene McCarthy in 1968 and organizing the Taxpayers' Campaign for Urban Priorities during the New York mayoral election of 1969.

Despite her broad-ranging activism, Abzug never stood for public office until 1970 when she decided to challenge Democratic incumbent Leonard Farbstein for the House seat from the Nineteenth District. Emphasizing the need for a more active representative in Congress, Abzug unseated Farbstein in the primary. In the general election against Republican-Liberal candidate Barry Farber she enlisted support from various groups with which she had worked over the years. She also enjoyed support from celebrity entertainers and Mayor John Lindsay. The national media focused on her successful campaign which foreshadowed the publicity she would attract as a sitting representative.

After her election Abzug announced her desire to sit on the Committee on Armed Services where no woman had been a member since Margaret Chase Smith in 1948. She was unable to overcome the objections of committee chairman F. Edward Hébert and was assigned to the Committee on Government Operations and the Committee on Public Works, but she made known her intention not to accept quietly the traditions of the House. On her first day in Congress, after taking her own "people's oath" on the steps of the Capitol, she introduced a resolution calling for the withdrawal of United States troops from Southeast Asia. During her first term she also called for an end to the draft, congressional approval of the Equal Rights Amendment, and an investigation into the competence of F.B.I. director J. Edgar Hoover.

The redistricting plan for New York eliminated Abzug's district in 1972. In order to hold on to her House seat she decided to challenge the popular reform Democrat William Fitts Ryan who had represented New York's Upper West Side for more than a decade and was an ally of many of Abzug's supporters. In a bitter campaign, even by the standards of New York City, Abzug lost the primary nomination to Ryan. In September, however, Ryan died, and the Democratic committee selected Abzug to take his place on the ticket. This time she faced Ryan's widow who ran on the Liberal Party ticket. Abzug won what turned out to be another heated and personal race.

Although Abzug easily won reelection in the Twentieth District in 1974, she declined to run again in 1976, opting to enter the Democratic primary for New York's open Senate seat. She lost that election to Daniel Patrick Moynihan and was also unsuccessful in her bid for the New York City mayoral nomination in 1977. When the winner of the mayor's race, Ed Koch, resigned from Congress, Abzug failed to win his vacant seat in the House. In her most recent attempt to return to Congress, Abzug established residency in Westchester County in order to challenge Republican incumbent Joseph DioGuardi, but she lost that bid as well.

MARYON PITTMAN ALLEN

United States Senator
Democrat of Alabama
Ninety-fifth Congress
June 8, 1978–November 7, 1978

Maryon Allen's brief Senate term was filled with controversy arising from her outspoken statements to the press and her attempt to win election to the remainder of her husband's term. She was born Maryon Pittman in Meridian, Mississippi, on November 30, 1925, and moved with her family to Birmingham, Alabama, the following year. After attending public schools and the University of Alabama, she worked as a journalist, editor, and lecturer.

As a reporter for the *Birmingham News*, Pittman interviewed Alabama's Lieutenant Governor James B. Allen in April 1964 following his speech before the Alabama Federation of Women's Clubs. They were married in August. Following her husband's election to the United States Senate in 1968, she wrote a

Washington-based column, entitled "The Reflections of a News Hen," syndicated in newspapers throughout Alabama. She was preparing a series of televised news commentaries at the time of her husband's death on June 1, 1978.

Governor George Wallace, for whom James Allen served as lieutenant governor in the 1960s, on June 8 appointed Maryon Allen to fill her husband's seat for an interim term until an election was held on November 7. Allen announced that she would also be a candidate for the remaining two years of her husband's term. Although Wallace, who was ineligible for reelection as governor, was expected to run for the Senate, he ruled himself out later in June.

Whatever support Wallace may have contributed to Allen's campaign evaporated in the wake of a Washington Post interview in which Allen was quoted as being highly critical of the governor and his wife. Allen later claimed the interview had distorted her comments, but the reaction in Alabama damaged her chances for election. Confident of victory, she concentrated on her Senate duties and campaigned little before the Democratic primary of September 5. She led the primary voting with 44 percent but was forced into a runoff with state senator Donald Stewart who defeated her by more than 120,000 votes in the runoff of September 26.

Allen later worked as a columnist for the *Washington Post* and is a public relations and advertising director for an antiques and decorating firm in Birmingham.

ELIZABETH BULLOCK ANDREWS

United States Representative
Democrat of Alabama
Ninety-second Congress
April 4, 1972–January 3, 1973

Elizabeth Andrews faced no Republican opposition after the Alabama Democratic Executive Committee selected her as the party's nominee for election to the vacancy left by the death of her husband, fifteen-term Representative George Andrews. Before the Committee named Andrews, she received the endorsement of Governor George Wallace, who announced his intention to back her as an independent candidate if the party failed to nominate her. Opposition to her candidacy came largely from black members of the Democratic Executive Committee.

Leslie Elizabeth Bullock was born in Geneva, Alabama, on February 12, 1911, and attended school in her hometown. In 1932 she graduated from Montevallo College and subsequently taught home economics. Her first introduction to politics came in 1944 when her husband, serving with the Navy in the Pacific, ran for Congress while she campaigned for him in Alabama.

In the Ninety-second Congress, Elizabeth Andrews served on the Committee on Post Office and Civil Service. She introduced several amendments to protect medical and Social Security benefits. With Rep. William Nichols she co-sponsored a bill establishing a Tuskegee Institute national historical park. Andrews declined to run for renomination for a full term. She is a resident of Union Springs, Alabama.

JEAN SPENCER ASHBROOK

(U.S. House of Representatives)

United States Representative
Republican of Ohio
Ninety-seventh Congress
June 29, 1982–January 3, 1983

Jean Ashbrook completed her husband's term of service in a House of Representatives seat that was soon to be eliminated through reapportionment and redistricting. John M. Ashbrook, after eleven terms as representative from Ohio's Seventeenth District, had entered the primary for Ohio's senatorial nomination before he died on April 24, 1982. Governor James A. Rhodes urged Jean Ashbrook to run in the special primary which she won on June 8. She went on to defeat Democratic candidate Jack Koelbe in the special election of June 29.

After being sworn in on July 12, 1982, Ashbrook served on the Committee on Merchant Marine and Fisheries. In July she introduced a bill that would have denied federal law enforcement or criminal justice assistance to any jurisdictions that implemented certain gun control ordinances. She also introduced a bill to prescribe mandatory minimum sentences for anyone convicted of federal felonies committed against senior citizens. Ashbrook supported the Enterprise Zone Tax Act of 1982, which provided tax relief and regulatory exemption for businesses that relocated to areas of high unemployment and poverty. She also supported a bill that would have created a United States Academy of Freedom to educate citizens about the dangers of communism and to promote democratic development in other countries.

Emily Jean Spencer was born in Cincinnati, Ohio, on September 21, 1934. After attending schools in Newark, Ohio, she received a B.S. from Ohio State University in 1956. She resides in Newark, Ohio.

IRENE BAILEY BAKER

United States Representative
Republican of Tennessee
Eighty-eighth Congress
March 10, 1964–January 3, 1965

Irene Baker served as Republican National Committeewoman from Tennessee for four years before she succeeded her husband in the House of Representatives in 1964. Soon after Howard H. Baker died in January 1964, the convention of Tennessee's Second District Republicans endorsed his widow, Irene Baker, as a candidate in the special election to fill the vacancy left by the death of the seven-term veteran of the House. Baker's low-key campaign emphasized her desire to continue her husband's work to achieve a balanced budget, to protect jobs in the district's nuclear laboratories and coal mines, and to support the Tennessee Valley Authority. In the election held March 10, Irene Baker defeated her Democratic opponent, Knoxville newspaperman, Willard Yarborough.

Before her election to the House, Baker had served in local government as a court clerk in Sevier County, Tennessee, from 1918 to 1924. She was a native of Sevier County where she was born Edith Irene Bailey in Sevierville on November 17, 1901, and where she attended school. Following her marriage to Howard Baker she worked in his political campaigns. She also served as chair of a state Republican committee to recruit new women voters.

After being sworn in as a Member of the House of Representatives on March 19, 1964, Baker served on the Committee on Government Operations. She advocated cost of living increases for Social Security recipients and criticized the Democratic administration for risking inflation through excessive governmental spending. Baker declined to seek renomination. She returned to Knoxville, Tennessee, where she worked as director of public welfare from 1965 to 1971. Her stepson, Howard H. Baker, Jr., served as U.S. senator from Tennessee from 1967 to 1985.

HELEN DELICH BENTLEY

(Office of Representative Bentley)

United States Representative
Republican of Maryland
Ninety-ninth–One Hundred First Congresses
January 3, 1985–present

As a Member of Congress, Helen Bentley has focused on the same economic issues that were at the center of her career as a journalist and federal appointee. Born in Ruth, Nevada, on November 28, 1923, she attended the University of Nevada and George Washington University before receiving her B.A. from the University of Missouri in 1944. Beginning in 1945, she was a reporter for the *Baltimore Sun*, covering the maritime industry of that port city and later covering labor and transportation issues as well. In addition to her newspaper work, Bentley produced a weekly television show focusing on Baltimore shipping and served as a consultant.

Bentley entered public service in 1969 when President Richard Nixon appointed her chairman of the Federal Maritime Commission where she served until 1975. She subsequently returned to work as a columnist for *World Port Magazine* and as an executive with a shipping company.

In 1984, as a Republican candidate for the House of Representatives, Bentley defeated long-time incumbent Clarence Long in Maryland's Second District. As she had in unsuccessful challenges to Long in 1980 and 1982, Bentley emphasized the need to improve Baltimore harbor in order to secure the economic health of the district. As a new representa-tive, Bentley gained seats on the Committee on Merchant Marine and Fisheries and the Committee on Public Works and Transportation. Beginning in the One Hundred First Congress, she took leave from Public Works and Transportation to serve on the Budget Committee. Bentley also serves on the Select Committee on Aging.

One of Bentley's central legislative achievements has been obtaining federal support for the dredging and improvement of Baltimore harbor. She also is particularly interested in legislation that protects American jobs and industry against foreign competition.

IRIS FAIRCLOTH BLITCH

United States Representative
Democrat of Georgia
Eighty-fourth–Eighty-seventh Congresses
January 3, 1955–January 3, 1963

Iris Faircloth was born near Vidalia, Georgia on April 25, 1912, and attended the public schools of Vidalia, Douglas, Fitzgerald and Homerville, Georgia, and of Hagerstown, Maryland. She was a student at the University of Georgia at Athens in 1929 and attended South Georgia College at Douglas in 1949. In October 1929 she married Brooks E. Blitch,

Jr., and worked with him in drug and naval stores businesses, pulpwood production and cattle and hog farming in Homerville.

Following an unsuccessful run for the Georgia General Assembly in 1940, Blitch was elected to the Georgia Senate in 1946 and to the state house of representatives in 1948. After her defeat for reelection in 1950 she was again elected to the state senate in 1952 and served until December 1954. She also served as secretary of the Georgia Democratic executive committee and represented Georgia on the Democratic National Committee.

Running as a supporter of Governor Herman Talmadge, Blitch defeated incumbent Representative William M. Wheeler in the September 1954 Democratic primary, a contest tantamount to election in Georgia's Eighth District. She was reelected three times.

In March 1956 Blitch joined ninety-five senators and representatives from eleven southern states in signing the "Southern Manifesto," which pledged the signatories to work to reverse the Supreme Court's 1954 decision outlawing racial segregation in public schools. Seeking to protect the jute-backing industry in her district and encourage the growth of industry throughout southern Georgia, Blitch favored amending the 1930 Tariff Act to make it more difficult for foreign-made jute to enter the country. In August 1961 she responded to attacks from Iowa Representative H.R. Gross and defended the use of the comic strip character "Pogo," a native of Georgia's Okefenokee Swamp and consequently her district, in a government pamphlet aimed at parents concerned with the television viewing habits of their children.

Because of ill health Blitch declined to run for renomination for a fifth term in 1962. In August 1964 she announced that she would leave the Democratic Party and support the Republican presidential candidacy of Senator Barry M. Goldwater.

Blitch is a resident of St. Simons Island, Georgia.

CORINNE CLAIBORNE (LINDY) BOGGS

(Office of Representative Boggs)

United States Representative
Democrat of Louisiana
Ninety-third–One Hundred First Congresses
March 20, 1973–present

When Lindy Boggs was elected to fill the seat of her late husband, she was thoroughly familiar with the world of both Capitol Hill and Louisiana politics. As the wife of a fourteen-term representative and majority leader of the House, Lindy Boggs played an active role in Hale Boggs' campaigns and in district politics. She has used that experience to build a legislative career of her own stretching over nine Congresses.

Born Corinne Morrison Claiborne at Brunswick Plantation, Louisiana, on March 13, 1916, Lindy Boggs graduated from Newcomb College of Tulane University in 1935 and taught high school history. She came to Washington when her husband won election to a single term in 1940 and when he returned to his seat in 1947. During Hale Boggs' service in the House, Lindy Boggs served as president of the Women's National Democratic Club, the Democratic Wives' Forum, and the Congressional Club. She chaired the inaugural committees for President Kennedy in 1961 and President Johnson in 1965, and in 1964 cochaired Lady Bird Johnson's whistle-stop campaign tour through the South. When the Ninety-third Congress declared Hale Boggs' seat vacant three months after his disappearance in an airplane over Alaska during a campaign trip in October 1972, Lindy Boggs won the seat in a special election held March 20, 1973. In her first term in Congress she served on the Committee on Banking and Currency and in the next Congress joined the Committee on House Administration. Beginning with the Ninety-fifth Congress she became a member of the Committee on Appropriations where she has served since with seats on the Subcommittees on Energy and Water Development, on the Legislative Branch, and on Veterans' Administration, Housing and Urban Development, and Independent Agencies. She also is a member of the Select Committee on Children, Youth and Families.

In 1976 Lindy Boggs became the first woman to preside over a national political convention when she served as chair of the Democratic National Convention. In addition to her legislative interest in housing policy, technological development, equal opportunities for women and minorities, and Mississippi River transportation, Boggs has worked to broaden interest in and awareness of American history. In 1976 she served as chair of the Joint Committee on Bicentennial Arrangements and served on the board of the American Revolution Bicentennial Administration. In the Ninety-ninth through One Hundred First Congresses, she chaired the Commission on the Bicentenary of the U.S. House of Representatives. She is also a member of the Commission on the Bicentennial of the United States Constitution. In July of 1987, she presided over a congressional ceremony at Independence Hall in Philadelphia in commemoration of the Great Compromise of the Federal Convention.

In July 1990, Lindy Boggs announced that she would not be a candidate for reelection to the One Hundred Second Congress. Her retirement marks a half century of combined congressional service with her husband.

VERONICA GRACE BOLAND

United States Representative
Democrat of Pennsylvania
Seventy-seventh Congress
November 3, 1942–January 3, 1943

After nomination by the executive committee of the Pennsylvania Democratic committee on June 5, 1942, Veronica Boland ran unopposed in a special election of November 3, 1942. She finished out the term of Patrick J. Boland, her late husband and majority whip of the House of Representatives. She was not a candidate in the election of the same day for representative from the Eleventh District of Pennsylvania for the succeeding Congress. Sworn in on November 19, 1942, Veronica Boland received no committee assignments for her short term and never participated in debate. Congress adjourned on December 16.

Born in Scranton on March 18, 1899, and educated at the Scranton Technical High

School, Veronica Grace Boland returned to her native city after resigning from Congress and worked as an executive secretary for a manufacturing company until 1957. She died in Scranton on June 19, 1982.

FRANCES PAYNE BOLTON

United States Representative
Republican of Ohio
Seventy-sixth–Ninetieth Congresses
February 27, 1940–January 3, 1969

The lengthy congressional career of Frances Bolton, like her earlier work in philanthropy, reflected a sense of patrician responsibility that she had developed as the daughter of a wealthy Ohio family at the turn of the century. She was born Frances Payne Bingham in Cleveland, Ohio, on March 29, 1885. She attended various schools including Miss Spence's School in New York City, although she received much of her education from private tutors as she travelled with her family. As a member of a debutante club in Cleveland she became involved with a visiting nurses' program in the city's tenements and began her lifelong interest in nursing and public health. She married Chester Bolton, a Cleveland lawyer, in 1907 and devoted most of her time to raising a family during the next ten years.

In 1917 Frances Bolton moved with her husband to Washington where he served on the War Industries Board and she worked with various nursing groups in support of the war effort. That same year she gained access to a trust fund established in her name by her uncle, Oliver Hazard Payne, a founder of Standard Oil and one of the nation's wealthiest men. The bequest made Bolton a very wealthy woman herself and allowed her to establish the Payne Fund which distributed grants that reflected her broad range of interests including nursing, children's literature, radio communication, and parapsychology.

For all her involvement in community affairs and philanthropic work, Bolton had no political experience before her husband was elected to the House of Representatives in 1928. After moving to Washington she became more directly involved in the political life of the capital and her husband's work as chairman of the Republican Congressional Committee in 1936. Following their return to Cleveland when Chester Bolton failed to win reelection in 1936, Frances served as a member of the Republican Central Committee of Ohio. Chester Bolton regained his House seat in 1938, and the Boltons returned to Washington for the opening of the Seventy-sixth Congress in January 1939. On October 29 of that year, Chester Bolton died, leaving a vacancy in Ohio's Twenty-second District.

Frances Bolton soon decided to seek her late husband's seat in Congress, and after winning the support of the Ohio Republican Party she received a larger vote than any her husband had enjoyed. As a member of the Seventy-sixth Congress, Bolton served on the Committee on Indian Affairs, the Committee on Expenditures in the Executive Depart-

ments, and the Committee on Election of the President, Vice President and Representatives. After her reelection to the succeeding Congress, she resigned her original assignments for a seat on the Committee on Foreign Affairs, where she served throughout her term in the House. Bolton entered Congress as an isolationist and critic of Roosevelt's New Deal. She opposed the Lend-Lease program to aid Britain and the Soviet Union before our entrance into the Second World War.

Once the United States entered the war, Bolton devoted much of her time to the familiar issue of nursing. The Bolton Act of 1943 created the U.S. Cadet Nurse Corps. She also traveled to military hospitals in Great Britain during 1944. In the years after the war she continued her travels as a member of the Foreign Affairs Committee, and following an appeal to Ambassador Andrei Gromyko, became the first committee member to travel to the Soviet Union.

Bolton, who was preceded in Congress by her grandfather, the Ohio representative and senator Henry B. Payne, as well as her husband, was joined in the Eighty-third, Eighty-fourth and Eighty-eighth Congresses by her son, Oliver Payne Bolton. His election marked the only time a mother and son have served in Congress concurrently. Frances Bolton maintained the popularity that had first carried her into office and by 1960 became the longest-serving woman then sitting in the House of Representatives and ranking Republican on Foreign Affairs. A large district staff, paid in part out of her own funds, helped provide services for her constituents. Finally, in 1968, Bolton lost a bid for reelection to seventerm Representative Charles Vanik when the two faced each other as a result of redistricting. She returned to Lyndhurst, Ohio, where she lived until her death there on March 9, 1977.

REVA ZILPHA BECK BOSONE

United States Representative
Democrat of Utah
Eighty-first–Eighty-second Congresses
January 3, 1949–January 3, 1953

"Her Honor—the Judge," Reva Bosone, was a diligent worker for the reclamation projects so important to Utah at the same time that she took numerous stands in defiance of public opinion in her largely conservative state. The great-granddaughter of Mormon pioneers, she was born in American Fork, Utah, on April 2, 1895. After attending public schools she graduated from Westminster Junior College in 1917 and received a B.A. from the University of California at Berkeley in 1919. From 1920 to 1927 she taught high school English and speech in American Fork, Delta, and Ogden, Utah. She attended the University of Utah College of Law at Salt Lake City and graduated in 1930. Beginning in 1931 she practiced law in Helper, Utah, and Salt Lake City.

In 1932 Bosone was elected to the state house of representatives. She was reelected in 1934 and the following year was elected majority leader. While in the legislature she worked to secure passage of a women's and children's wage and hour law and a child labor amendment to the State constitution. In 1936 she was elected a police and traffic court judge of the Salt Lake City Municipal Court and served until she ran for Congress. While on the bench she did not hesitate to issue harsh fines for convicted drunk drivers at the same time that she took a personal interest in rehabilitating offenders. During the Second World War she was chair of the Women's Army Corps Civilian Advisory Committee of the Ninth Service Command and was an official observer at the United Nations' founding conference at San Francisco in 1945. During 1947 and 1948 Bosone served as the first director of the Utah State Board for Education on Alcoholism.

In 1948 Bosone was elected to represent Utah's Second District over a Republican freshman incumbent, William A. Dawson. In 1950 she won a second term over Republican National committeewoman and future Treasurer of the United States, Ivy Baker Priest. In her freshman term, Bosone served on the Committee on Public Lands and in the succeeding Congress was appointed to the Committee on House Administration and the Committee on Interior and Insular Affairs. During her first term she tried to encourage Native American self-government by introducing a bill to reduce gradually federal administration of Indian affairs. She favored extension of Social Security, funding for public housing for military personnel, and statehood for Hawaii and Alaska. Bosone voted against the Subversive Activities Control and Communist Registration Act and the 1949 Central Intelligence Agency Act.

Bosone hoped to promote land management and reclamation efforts through her proposed Small Water Projects bill which would have established a revolving fund to pay for modest reclamation projects. She attempted to include the proposed Echo Park Dam as part of the Colorado River Project despite opposition from conservation groups. She also aided the unsuccessful effort to authorize construction of Hell's Canyon dam on Idaho's Snake River.

Bosone was defeated for a third term in 1952 in a rematch with William Dawson. The campaign provoked charges that she was sympathetic to communism and had received $630 in kickbacks in 1950 from two staff members. (Bosone claimed to have signed the campaign disclosure form without noticing the listing of the donation. The money was never spent and was later found in her office safe.)

Bosone tried to regain her seat in 1954 but again lost to Dawson. She resumed the practice of law in Salt Lake City until 1957 when she became legal counsel to the safety and compensation subcommittee of the House Committee on Education and Labor and served there until 1960. The arrival of a Democratic administration in 1961 offered the prospect of appointment as assistant interior secretary or commissioner of Indian affairs, but instead she was named the Post Office Department's judicial officer and chair of its contract board of appeals. She held this post until her retirement in January 1968. Bosone lived in Vienna, Virginia, until her death there on July 21, 1983.

EVA KELLY BOWRING

United States Senator
Republican of Nebraska
Eighty-third Congress
April 16, 1954–November 7, 1954

Eva Bowring served for eight years as vice chair of the Nebraska Republican Central Committee and director of women's activities for the Nebraska Republican Party before serving in the United States Senate. Governor Robert B. Crosby appointed Bowring on April 16, 1954, to fill the vacancy caused by the death of Senator Dwight Griswold. She was sworn in on April 26 for the term that would end, according to Nebraska law, at the next general election when a candidate would be selected to finish out the final two months of Griswold's term.

Bowring served on the Committee on Interstate and Foreign Commerce, the Committee on Labor and Public Welfare, and the Committee on Post Office and Civil Service. In her first speech on the Senate floor, she declared her support for a program of flexible agricultural price supports proposed by the Eisenhower administration. She and Nebraska's other senator, Hugh A. Butler, introduced a bill for the construction of the Red Willow Dam and Reservoir as part of the Missouri River Basin project. Bowring also sponsored legislation providing for flood control works in the Gering Valley of Nebraska.

The needs of Nebraska's agricultural constituents were familiar to Bowring who continued to work the 10,000 acre cattle ranch that she and her late husband developed. She was born in Nevada, Missouri, on January 9, 1892. Her first husband died in 1924, and after remarrying in 1928 she moved to Arthur

Bowring's ranch near Merriman in the Sandhill country of Nebraska. In addition to her ranch work, she became involved in local Republican politics and in the Nebraska Stockgrowers Association.

In June 1954 Bowring announced that she would not seek election to the short term to follow the November general election. She was succeeded by another woman and a Republican, Hazel Abel. After retirement from the Senate, Bowring served on the national advisory council of the National Institutes of Health from 1954 to 1958 and in 1960 and 1961. She was on the board of parole of the Department of Justice from 1956 to 1964. Bowring died in Gordon, Nebraska, on January 8, 1985.

BARBARA BOXER

(Office of Representative Boxer)

United States Representative
Democrat of California
Ninety-eighth–One Hundred First Congresses
January 3, 1983–present

Barbara Boxer arrived as a Member of the House of Representatives with experience as both a congressional staff assistant and a local officeholder in her California district. Born Barbara Levy in Brooklyn, N.Y., on November 11, 1940, she graduated from Brooklyn College with a B.A. in 1962 and worked as a stockbroker and newspaper journalist in

California before joining the district staff of Congressman John L. Burton in 1974. In 1976 she won election to the Marin County (California) Board of Supervisors and in 1981 became the first woman president of the Board.

When John Burton announced his retirement from Congress in 1982, Boxer announced her candidacy for the seat of her former employer. With the endorsement of Burton, she won the Democratic nomination over five other candidates and went on to win election from California's Sixth District which encompasses Marin County, part of San Francisco, and parts of Solano and Sonoma Counties.

Boxer has served on the Committee on Government Operations and the Committee on Merchant Marine and Fisheries as well as the Budget Committee and Armed Services Committee. She is also a member of the Select Committee on Children, Youth and Families and co-chair of the Military Reform Caucus.

Boxer's committee assignments have offered her the opportunity to promote congressional oversight of executive branch spending, particularly in defense programs. She played a leading role in the exposure of Pentagon procurement scandals and has worked to ensure greater accountability from the military. Other legislative priorities include health care, especially federal funding of the fight against AIDS and the fight for a woman's right to choose.

VERA DAERR BUCHANAN

(U.S. House of Representatives)

United States Representative
Democrat of Pennsylvania
Eighty-second–Eighty-fourth Congresses
July 24, 1951–November 26, 1955

Vera Daerr was born in Wilson, (later a part of Clairton) Pennsylvania, on July 20, 1902, and subsequently moved to Duquesne, Pennsylvania, where she attended the public and parochial schools. In 1929 she married Frank Buchanan, a school teacher who was elected mayor of McKeesport in 1942. Vera Buchanan operated a beauty shop in McKees-

port and was a member of the Democratic Women's Guild. Her husband was elected a representative from Pennsylvania's Thirty-third District in a May 1946 special election.

Following Frank Buchanan's death on April 27, 1951, Vera Buchanan, who had served as his secretary, was nominated to take his place. She won a special election held July 24,

1951, defeating the Republican nominee, McKeesport city controller Clifford W. Flegal, who had been sharply critical of President Truman and the foreign policy of Secretary of State Dean Acheson.

When Pennsylvania lost three house seats as a result of the 1950 Census, Buchanan's district became the Thirtieth, but she twice won reelection with wide margins provided by her overwhelmingly Democratic, pro-labor constituency.

Buchanan was sworn in as a member of the Eighty-third Congress on August 1, 1951, and served on the Committee on Merchant Marine and Fisheries, the Committee on Banking and Currency, and the Committee on Public Works. A solid supporter of the Truman administration, she was an advocate of housing legislation and a proponent of the Turtle Creek Valley Flood Control Project. She also was an ardent defender of unions and the rights of laborers.

Buchanan died in McKeesport on November 26, 1955.

YVONNE BRATHWAITE BURKE

(U.S. House of Representatives)

United States Representative
Democrat of California
Ninety-third–Ninety-fifth Congresses
January 3, 1973–January 3, 1979

Yvonne Burke gained national attention several months before her election to the House of Representatives when as vice-chair of the Democratic National Convention in July 1972 she even-handedly presided over a stormy consideration of the party platform. One month earlier she defeated four rivals for the Democratic nomination for Congress, and in November defeated the Republican to win the seat representing California's newly-created Thirty-seventh District.

Burke already had established herself as a well-known figure in California politics and in her Los Angeles law practice. She was born Perle Yvonne Watson in Los Angeles on October 5, 1932. She attended Berkeley and graduated from the University of California at Los Angeles with a B.A. in political science in 1953. Three years later she received a J.D. from the University of Southern California School of Law and entered practice in her native city. In addition to her private practice, she served in numerous other capacities such as the state's deputy corporation commissioner, attorney on the staff of the McCone Commission established to investigate the Watts riots, and a hearing officer for the Los Angeles Police Commission. From 1967 to 1972 she served as the first black woman in the California legislature.

In her first term in Congress, Burke served on the Committee on Interior and Insular Affairs and in December 1974 transferred to the Committee on Appropriations on which she served throughout her term. As a member of Appropriations she called for additional federal funding of community nutrition programs. She also sought funding for the resettlement of Vietnamese refugees and supported the Humphrey-Hawkins bill for full employment. Burke was one of several Members who in 1977 secured a human rights amendment to the foreign aid bill, and she supported other such efforts to pressure foreign governments guilty of human rights violations. She also worked to restore planning grants from Housing and Urban Development. In 1977 she introduced the Displaced Homemakers Act which authorized job training centers for women entering the labor market.

Burke was selected as the first woman to chair the Congressional Black Caucus in 1976.

In 1978 Burke declined to run for reelection to Congress, seeking instead to become California attorney general. After failing to win that election she gained an appointment to the Los Angeles County Board of Supervisors and served on that panel from June 1979 until her resignation in December 1980. She continues to practice law in Los Angeles.

SALA BURTON

United States Representative
Democrat of California
Ninety-eighth–One-Hundredth Congresses
June 21, 1983–February 1, 1987

Sala Burton was elected to the House of Representatives from California's Fifth District in a special election held on June 21, 1983, to fill the vacancy left by the death of her husband, Phillip Burton. From the time that she met Phillip Burton at a convention of Young Democrats in 1950 and married him three years later, Sala Burton followed an active political career that paralleled her husband's rise to influence in Congress. She was a founder of the California Democratic Council and served as its vice president from 1951 to 1954. Burton served as president of the San Francisco Democratic Women's Forum from 1957 to 1959 and was a member of both the San Francisco County and California State

Democratic Central Committees. In Washington she served as president of the Democratic Wives of the House and Senate from 1972 to 1974.

Sala Galante was born in Bialystok, Poland, on April 1, 1925. With her parents she fled from Poland in 1939, just before the Nazi invasion and occupation. She attended public schools in San Francisco and the San Francisco University. From 1949 to 1950 she was associate director of the California Public Affairs Institute. In addition to her political party activity, Burton worked with the NAACP in its efforts to eliminate job and housing discrimination.

Eight days after the death of her husband Sala Burton announced that she was a candidate for his seat. In the special election she gained a clear majority in a field of eleven candidates and avoided a runoff. In the Ninety-eighth Congress she was appointed to her husband's former seats on the Committee on Education and Labor and the Committee on Interior and Insular Affairs. She also served on the Select Committee on Hunger. In the Ninety-ninth Congress, after failing in a hard-fought effort to win a seat on Appropriations, she was named to the Committee on Rules.

From her committee assignments, Burton was able to serve as an advocate for a broad range of policies such as social welfare programs, child nutrition assistance, bilingual education, and the Equal Rights Amendment. She also spoke in defense of Soviet dissidents. After her reelection to the One-Hundredth Congress, Burton was too ill to take the oath of office on the House floor and was sworn in at her home. On February 1, 1987, she died in Washington.

VERA CAHALAN BUSHFIELD

United States Senator
Republican of South Dakota
Eightieth Congress
October 6, 1948–December 26, 1948

Vera Bushfield's brief Senate service in the autumn of 1948 never brought her to Washington, where the Eightieth Congress had recessed for the remainder of the election year. She stayed in her native South Dakota to concentrate on constituent services during the last three months of her late husband's term. Senator Harlan J. Bushfield died September 27, 1948, after announcing earlier in the year that he did not intend to run for reelection in November. Governor George T. Mickelson appointed Vera Bushfield to fill out the term while a successor was chosen in the general election. She resigned her seat six days before the end of the Eightieth Congress so that Karl Mundt, the victor in the November election, might gain seniority by filling out the final days of Bushfield's term.

The Senate was the first and only official public service for Vera Bushfield who served as South Dakota's first lady when her husband was governor from 1939 to 1943. She was born in Miller, South Dakota, on August 9, 1889, and graduated from the Stout Institute in Menominee, Wisconsin, in 1912. She also attended Dakota Wesleyan University and the University of Minnesota. She died in Fort Collins, Colorado, on April 16, 1976.

BEVERLY BUTCHER BYRON

(Office of Representative Byron)

United States Representative
Democrat of Maryland
Ninety-sixth–One Hundred First Congress
January 3, 1979–present

Beverly Byron has taken a leading interest in armed services legislation in the twelve years since she was elected to fill the seat held by her late husband. She joined the Committee on Armed Services during her first term in office and by 1987 gained the chair of the Subcommittee on Military Personnel and

Compensation. She is the first woman to chair an Armed Services subcommittee.

Beverly Butcher was born in Baltimore on July 27, 1932, and grew up in Washington, D.C., where her father served in the military, including duty as an aide to General Eisenhower during the Second World War. She attended Hood College, and following her marriage to Goodloe E. Byron she worked in his campaign for the Maryland legislature and in 1970 for the U.S. House of Representatives. When Goodloe Byron died one month before the general election in 1978, Beverly Byron agreed to run for his seat from Maryland's Sixth District, and she won easily. Beverly Byron succeeded her husband in office just as his mother, Katharine E. Byron, had succeeded his father, William D. Byron, following the latter's death in 1941.

In addition to her seat on Armed Services, Beverly Byron is a member of the Committee on Interior and Insular Affairs and the Select Committee on Aging. She served as chair of the House Special Panel on Arms Control and Disarmament from 1983 to 1986. While her most important focus has been on military and defense legislation, Byron has also taken an interest in the promotion of physical fitness and improvement of national recreational areas. She served as chairman of the Maryland Commission on Physical Fitness from 1979 to 1989 and was a member of the board of the American Hiking Society.

KATHARINE EDGAR BYRON

(U.S. House of Representatives)

United States Representative
Democrat of Maryland
Seventy-seventh Congress
May 27, 1941–January 3, 1943

Katharine Byron entered the House of Representatives through a special election held on the eve of the United States entry into the Second World War. Her husband, William D. Byron, was killed in an airplane accident on February 27, 1941, less than two months after the beginning of his second term in Congress. In the special election held May 27, 1941, to fill the vacant seat from Maryland's Sixth District, Katharine Byron narrowly defeated Republican A. Charles Stewart in a contest that centered on the nation's response to war in Europe. In campaign appearances with nationally-known Democrats like Representative Estes Kefauver and First Lady Eleanor Roosevelt, Byron endorsed American support for nations fighting against the Nazis and recommended greater military preparedness for this nation.

Byron was sworn in as a member of the Seventy-seventh Congress on June 11, 1941, and served on the Committee on the Civil Service and the Committee on War Claims. In a debate on amendment of the Neutrality Act in November 1941, Byron urged her colleagues to accelerate the delivery of war materiel to Great Britain and the Soviet Union. The same month she christened the Liberty Fleet freighter *Francis Scott Key* at a Baltimore shipyard. On the day following the Japanese attack on Pearl Harbor, Speaker Sam Rayburn designated Byron and four other representatives to declare on the House floor their support for a declaration of war.

Following General Douglas MacArthur's defense of the Philippines in 1942, Byron introduced an amendment to include the Maryland extension of the Conduit Road in a proposal to change the Washington, D.C. portion of the road to MacArthur Boulevard. That same year she argued for the maintenance of Works Projects Administration programs as a necessary adjunct to national defense projects.

Katharine Edgar was born in Detroit, Michigan, on October 25, 1903, and attended schools in Connecticut and Washington, D.C. As a resident of Williamsport, Maryland, after her marriage, Byron was active in Red Cross projects and served as town commissioner from 1938 to 1940. Although Byron initially filed for reelection in 1942, in August she withdrew as a candidate, citing her wish to spend more time with her five sons. She continued to work with the Red Cross in Washington where she died on December 28, 1976. Her son, Goodloe E. Byron, served in the House of Representatives from 1971 to 1978, and he, like, his father was succeeded upon his death by his wife, Beverly Byron.

HATTIE WYATT CARAWAY

United States Senator
Democrat of Arkansas
Seventy-second–Seventy-eighth Congresses
November 13, 1931–January 2, 1945

The first woman elected to the United States Senate, Hattie Caraway was born Hattie Ophelia Wyatt in Bakerville, Tennessee, on February 1, 1878. After attending public schools and graduating from Dickson (Tennessee) Normal College in 1896, she married Thaddeus Horatius Caraway in February 1902 and moved with him to Jonesboro, Arkansas.

Thaddeus Caraway was elected to the House of Representatives in 1912 and to the Senate in 1920. Following Caraway's death on November 6, 1931, Arkansas Governor Harvey Parnell appointed Hattie Caraway to fill the vacancy until a special election for the remainder of Thaddeus Caraway's term was held in January 1932. Although Caraway won the special election, she was given little chance to win the August 1932 primary for the full six-year term against four opponents, including former Governor Charles H. Brough and former Senator William F. Kirby. Her opportunities improved overnight when Senator Huey P. Long entered the campaign on Caraway's behalf. The charismatic Louisianan effectively portrayed her as a champion of poor white farmers and workers and as a Senator whom monied interests were unable to control. Long genuinely sympathized with Caraway and, with an eye to his possible candidacy for president, was eager to demonstrate that his popularity extended beyond Louisiana. He also hoped to humiliate and frighten Caraway's Arkansas colleague, Senate minority leader Joseph T. Robinson, a zealous enemy of Long. Caraway easily won the primary and was elected in November, defeating independent candidate Rex Floyd.

Although it was rare for Caraway to participate in debate or deliver a speech on the Senate floor, she eventually gained respect as a conscientious senator who generally supported the foreign policy and the domestic economic program of President Roosevelt and was attentive to the needs of her largely agri-cultural constituency. She was particularly interested in farm relief and flood control. She was a prohibitionist, a critic of lobbying groups, a friend of veterans and a co-sponsor of a proposed Equal Rights Amendment to the Constitution. Like most of her southern colleagues she opposed the anti-lynching law of 1938 and a proposed bill of 1942 to eliminate the poll tax.

At the opening of the Seventy-third Congress in 1933, Caraway was elected chair of the Committee on Enrolled Bills and served in that position until she left the Senate in 1945. She also served on the Committee on Agriculture and Forestry and the Committee on Commerce. In 1938 Caraway won renomination by narrowly defeating Sixth District Representative John L. McClellan, who would later serve Arkansas in the Senate for thirty-four years. She ran for renomination to a third term in 1944 but finished last in a four-candidate race won by Third District Representative J. William Fulbright. Shortly after her legislative career ended she was nominated by Roosevelt and confirmed by the Senate as a member of the Employees' Compensation Commission on which she served from 1946 to 1950. She died in Falls Church, Virginia, on December 21, 1950.

SHIRLEY ANITA CHISHOLM

United States Representative
Democrat of New York
Ninety-first–Ninety-seventh Congresses
January 3, 1969–January 3, 1983

In 1968 a court-ordered reapportionment of New York's congressional districts created a new Twelfth District centered in the Bedford-Stuyvesant section of Brooklyn. A community activist and member of the state legislature, Shirley Chisholm, won the election in that district to become the first black woman to serve in Congress. For fourteen years, Chis-

holm served in the House of Representatives as a champion of her constituents, some of the poorest in the nation, and a widely recognized advocate of liberal social causes.

Shirley Anita St. Hill was born in Brooklyn on November 30, 1924, and as a young girl lived with her grandparents in Barbados where she attended school. She graduated from high school after returning to Brooklyn and received her B.A. from Brooklyn College in 1946. She received her M.A. from Columbia University in 1952. Chisholm worked as a school teacher after her graduation from college and later was director of two child care centers. She also served as an educational consultant for New York's Division of Day Care. After years of community service, Chisholm entered elective politics as a member of the New York legislature in 1964 and served there until she ran for Congress.

Chisholm, declaring her motto "unbought and unbossed," narrowly won the Democratic primary for the House seat from the Twelfth District in 1968, running against two candidates, a man and a woman. She went on to defeat James Farmer, a civil rights activist and former chairman of the Congress on Racial Equality who was the nominee of the Republican and Liberal parties. When Chisholm arrived in the House from her inner-city district, the Democratic members of the Ways and Means Committee assigned her to the Committee on Agriculture. Chisholm, already a critic of the committee system and its emphasis on seniority, appealed to the party caucus for reassignment to a committee of greater relevance to her district. She received a seat on the Committee on Veterans' Affairs and in the Ninety-second through Ninety-fourth Congresses served on the Committee on Education and Labor. In the Ninety-fifth through Ninety-seventh Congresses she was a member of the influential Rules Committee. Chisholm also served on the Committee on Organization Study and Review which recom-

mended the reforms in the selection process for committee chairmen that were adopted by the Democratic Caucus in 1971.

Throughout her service in Congress, Chisholm fought to extend or protect the same kind of social programs that were at the center of her community activism and state political experience. Among her efforts to aid families were her proposed funding increases to extend the hours of day-care facilities and open such facilities to the children of working mothers of low and middle income, sponsorship of the Adequate Income Act of 1971 which guaranteed an annual income for families, and her defense of the Office of Economic Opportunity against the Nixon administration's efforts to eliminate the agency.

Chisholm spoke out on a wide variety of issues of importance during her years in office. In her first term, she joined fifteen colleagues in introducing legislation to end the draft and create a volunteer armed force. From her earliest days in Congress she fought for reductions in defense spending. Chisholm called for an end to British arms sales to South Africa. She was a staunch defender of federal assistance to education.

In 1972 Shirley Chisholm declared her candidacy for the Democratic nomination for president. She campaigned throughout the country and was on the ballot in twelve primaries in what was largely an educational campaign. In 1982, Chisholm announced that she would not be a candidate for reelection to the House. She is a resident of Williamsville, New York.

MARGUERITE STITT CHURCH

United States Representative
Republican of Illinois
Eighty-second–Eighty-seventh Congresses
January 3, 1951–January 3, 1963

After years assisting the political career of her husband and working in various charity activities, Marguerite Stitt Church was elected to the House of Representatives in 1950 to fill the seat formerly held by her husband. A popular congresswoman known for her personal attention to constituent services, she served for twelve years before imposing retirement on herself at the age of seventy. Until her death at ninety-eight she remained active in political campaigns and the volunteer work that had long engaged her.

Marguerite Stitt was born in New York City on September 13, 1892. She graduated from Wellesley College in 1914 and taught there for a year before enrolling in a masters program in political science at Columbia University. After completing her graduate degree she worked for a year as a consulting psychologist with the State Charities Aid Association of New York City. In 1918 she married Illinois state legislator Ralph Church and moved to Evanston, Illinois. There she worked in a succession of organizations devoted to family and children's welfare.

When Ralph Church was elected to the House of Representatives in 1934, Marguerite became more closely involved in his political career. In addition to campaigning for him, she frequently accompanied him on investigative trips. She embarked on her own speaking tours as part of the Republican presidential campaigns in 1940 and 1944. During and after the Second World War she made several inspection tours of Europe at the request of her husband. In Washington she served as president of the Congressional Club.

Ralph Church died in the midst of a House committee hearing in March 1950, and party leaders in Illinois persuaded Marguerite to run for election to his seat in the Thirteenth District. In the general election of November 1950, she won the first of six terms. As a freshman she was appointed to the Committee on Expenditures in the Executive Departments (before which her husband had died), and in the following Congress sat on the Committee on Government Operations and the Committee on Foreign Affairs which was to be her assignment through the remainder of her service. As a member of Foreign Affairs, she traveled extensively, particularly in Asia. While on Government Operations she worked for enactment of the recommendations offered by the Second Hoover Commission on efficiency in government. Church helped pass the act that placed the federal budget on a system of annual expenditures.

In 1962 Church voluntarily withdrew from elective politics. After retirement from Congress she served on the national board of directors for the Girl Scouts of America and on the board of the U.S. Capitol Historical Society. She worked for the presidential campaigns of Goldwater in 1964 and Nixon in 1968. Church died in Evanston on May 26, 1990.

MARIAN WILLIAMS CLARKE

United States Representative
Republican of New York
Seventy-third Congress
December 28, 1933–January 3, 1935

Republican Marian Clarke entered the House of Representatives in the first Congress of the New Deal when she won the special election of December 28, 1933, held to fill the vacancy in the Thirty-fourth District left by the death of her husband, John D. Clarke. She easily won the election over a Binghamton council member in the heavily Republican district. As a member of the Seventy-third Congress, however, she faced the frustrations of the minority party in an overwhelmingly Democratic House of Representatives. Clarke served on the Committee on Civil Service, the Committee on Claims, and the Committee on Invalid Pensions. In her year of service, she introduced a measure to restore reductions in the equipment allowance for rural mail carriers and urged the amendment of the Tariff Act of 1930 to protect the shoe manufacturers in her district from inferior products imported from foreign countries.

Clarke had hoped to carry on the legislative work of her husband who had served during six Congresses. Following his death in an automobile accident, she was nominated on the eleventh ballot by the district's Republican committee. She announced her intention to run for reelection in 1934 but withdrew before the primary, thus ending her first and last involvement in elective politics. Clarke was born Marian Williams on July 29, 1880, in Standing Stone, Pennsylvania, and after moving to Cheyenne, Wyoming as a young girl, grew up in various western states. She attended art school at the University of Nebraska and graduated from Colorado College in 1902. After working for a newspaper in Colorado Springs, she married and moved to Delaware County, New York. Upon her retirement from the House, she returned to her farm near Dehli, New York, and lived there until she died in Cooperstown, New York, on April 8, 1953.

CARDISS COLLINS

(Office of Representative Collins)

United States Representative
Democrat of Illinois
Ninety-third–One Hundred First Congresses
June 5, 1973–present

After winning the special election to fill the vacancy left by the death of her husband in 1973, Cardiss Collins has gone on to become the longest serving black woman in the history of Congress. Her seniority in office has allowed her to concentrate on the issues important to her district on the west side of Chicago

and to develop expertise in the legislation associated with her committee service.

Cardiss H. Robertson was born September 24, 1931, in St. Louis, Missouri, and grew up there and in Detroit. She attended Northwestern University and remained in Chicago where she worked for the Illinois Department of Labor and later the Illinois Department of

Revenue. She worked for the latter office as an auditor until her election to Congress.

Collins gained her first political experience in the party organization of Chicago when she served as committeewoman of the Twenty-fourth Ward Regular Democratic Organization. She also participated in her husband's various campaigns for alderman, committeeman, and U.S. Representative. Shortly after George Collins won election to his second term in Congress, he died in an airplane crash in Chicago in December 1972. Cardiss Collins won the special election to fill the seat on June 5, 1973.

Collins' longest committee service has been with the Committee on Government Oper-ations where she is the ranking Democrat and served first as chair of the Subcommittee on Manpower and Housing and now as chair of the Subcommittee on Government Activities and Transportation. In the latter position she has been at the forefront of congressional efforts to increase airport security and air safety. Collins served on the Committee on International Relations (later Foreign Affairs) from 1975 to 1980 and since 1981 has been a member of the Committee on Energy and Commerce. She also sits on the Select Committee on Narcotics Abuse and Control.

In 1979 Collins served as chair of the Congressional Black Caucus. She is the first black and the first woman to serve as a Democratic whip-at-large.

EMILY TAFT DOUGLAS

(U.S. House of Representatives)

United States Representative
Democrat of Illinois
Seventy-ninth Congress
January 3, 1945–January 3, 1947

Emily Taft Douglas of Illinois recognized the dangers of fascism during the mid-1930s and dedicated her public career to the cause of collective security against aggression and the establishment of a permanent machinery to insure international peace. The daughter of sculptor Laredo Taft, she was born in Chicago on April 10, 1899, and was graduated with a B.A. from the University of Chicago in 1920. Following study at the American Academy of Dramatic Art she worked in the theater and by 1926 was the star of *The Cat and the Canary* on Broadway.

In 1931 she married University of Chicago professor Paul H. Douglas, who at the age of fifty enlisted as a Marine private in 1942 and later was elected to three terms as senator from Illinois. Disturbed by the rise of fascism in Europe and by the Italian invasion of Ethiopia, she returned from a trip abroad in 1935 to organize and chair the Illinois League of Women Voters' department of government and foreign policy. In 1942 she became executive secretary of the International Relations Center in Chicago.

In February 1944 Illinois Democrats chose Douglas as their nominee for the state's at-large seat in the House of Representatives. In the general election, Douglas, who ran as a supporter of Roosevelt's foreign polices, faced Republican Stephen A. Day, one of the staunchest isolationists in the House. Despite the formidable opposition of the *Chicago Tribune* and its powerful publisher, Colonel Robert McCormick, she defeated Day by over 191,000 votes.

Shortly after the opening of the Seventy-ninth Congress and in her first House vote, Douglas opposed the establishment of a standing Committee on Un-American Activities. She also helped rescue former Vice President Henry Wallace's chances to become secretary of commerce by acceding to the demands of Wallace's opponents and voting for legislation to withdraw the Reconstruction Finance Corporation's lending bureau from the jurisdiction of the Commerce Department.

During her term in the Seventy-ninth Congress Douglas served on the Committee on Foreign Affairs and was widely recognized as a specialist in the field. She joined several committee colleagues on a visit to Europe in August 1945 to inspect the work of the United Nations Relief and Rehabilitation Administration. Along with California Representative Jerry Voorhis, she proposed legislation to put the United Nations in charge of international programs for arms control and the abolition of atomic weaponry. She also called for greater federal support for libraries, particularly those in rural and low-income areas, and co-sponsored a public library service demonstration bill.

Weary and frustrated by wartime controls and shortages and the strains of demobilization, voters in the mid-term elections of 1946 ousted fifty-four House Democrats, among them Douglas who lost to William G. Stratton. Following her husband's election to the Senate in 1948, she served on the legislative committee of the Unitarian Fellowship for Social Justice and as vice president of the American Unitarian Association. Douglas also wrote a book for juveniles, a biography of Margaret Sanger and a book of biographical essays on famous American women. She is a resident of White Plains, New York.

HELEN GAHAGAN DOUGLAS

(U.S. House of Representatives)

United States Representative
Democrat of California
Seventy-ninth–Eighty-first Congresses
January 3, 1945–January 3, 1951

After achieving early success as a stage actress and opera singer, Helen Gahagan Douglas embraced politics with the vitality and determination that characterized her career as a performer. Raised in an affluent, Republican family, she became the most ardent of converts to the New Deal and championed the policies of Roosevelt in the post-war years and the early days of the Cold War. Her uncompromising adherence to liberal ideals isolated her from many Democrats in the late 1940s and contributed to the first serious disappointment of her life when in 1950 she lost to Richard Nixon in one of the most celebrated Senate campaigns in American history.

Born on November 25, 1900, in Boonton, New Jersey, Helen Gahagan grew up in the fashionable Park Slope section of Brooklyn, New York. She attended boarding school in Northampton, Massachusetts, and returned to New York City to enroll at Barnard College where she became interested in the theater. Against the wishes of her father she took a part in a Broadway show and achieved overnight fame. Gahagan abandoned her college studies and throughout the 1920s appeared in a succession of popular shows and at the same time entered into another career as an opera singer. In 1931, while appearing on Broadway in *Tonight or Never*, she married her co-star, Melvyn Douglas.

Her marriage to a politically astute actor and the couple's move to California marked the beginning of Helen Douglas's political awareness. During the cross-country trip she was inspired to help alleviate the problems of migrant farm families and was later active with the John Steinbeck Committee that assisted the farm workers. In the midst of film acting and continued concert appearances, she became involved in a variety of political causes in the 1930s. After a concert tour of Europe in 1937 exposed her to the intensity of Nazi anti-semitism, she returned to California and with her husband helped organize members of the film industry in anti-fascist organizations and German boycotts.

In 1940 Douglas was elected a Democratic National Committeewoman from California and attended her first Democratic National Convention. As leading Democrats in the film industry, she and her husband became close friends of the Roosevelts and were guests at the White House. She served on the presidential advisory panels for the Works Progress Administration and the National Youth Administration. Helen Douglas so impressed the president with her support for his programs and her energetic party activity that he persuaded her to run for Congress from California's Fourteenth District in 1944.

Douglas not only won the seat from the economically and racially diverse Los Angeles district, she gained a rare freshman appointment to the Committee on Foreign Affairs.

From that seat she made clear her support of the United Nations, the Marshall Plan, the Bretton Woods agreements, and the independence of the Philippines. In domestic affairs she supported organized labor and sought better housing. She was chief House sponsor of the McMahon-Douglas act that established civilian control of atomic energy.

As representative of the largest black neighborhood in the West, Douglas insisted on equal rights for all Americans. She was the first white representative to hire black staff, appointed black constituents to West Point, and helped desegregate dining facilities in the Capitol. After John Rankin of Mississippi claimed on the House floor that black troops were responsible for widespread American fatalities in key battles of the Second World War, Douglas drew on Army and Navy records to prepare an extended address on black military achievements and heroism during the war.

Douglas's tireless support of New Deal social legislation and her promotion of Roosevelt's vision of international relations in the post-war era drew fire from various critics. She clashed with Secretary of State Dean Acheson over her strong support of Israeli independence and broke with Truman by voting against military aid to Greece and Turkey. In response to John Rankin's insinuation that she was a communist sympathizer, she delivered on the House floor "My Democratic Credo" which asserted that communism was not a serious threat to American democratic institutions but demagoguery and false charges were.

After three terms in the House, Douglas decided to seek the Senate seat held by Democrat Sheridan Downey. The incumbent withdrew before the primary, and in the general election Douglas faced another representative, Republican Richard Nixon, already famed as an anti-communist for his role in the Alger Hiss case. The candidates offered sharply contrasting visions of the post-war United States and its role in the world. The bitterly personal campaign, however, did little to explore the issues. In the most famous of the "dirty tricks" which established a reputation the Republican candidate never escaped, Nixon's staff prepared a review of Douglas's voting record and emphasized the similarities with New York's leftist Representative Vito Marcantonio. Thousands of copies of the flier were printed on pink paper and distributed throughout the state. Almost all of the 354 votes cited on the celebrated "pink sheet" were shared by the Democratic majority as well as Douglas and Marcantonio, and many conservative Republicans voted with the isolationist Marcantonio on foreign policy questions, but Nixon's allegations found a receptive audience among voters frightened by the recent communist invasion of South Korea and placed Douglas on the defensive for the remainder of the campaign. She was also the victim of anti-semitic attacks led by Gerald L.K. Smith. Anonymous phone calls to thousands of voters alleged that Douglas was a communist and reminded listeners that her husband was Jewish.

The political career of Douglas ended with her loss to Richard Nixon. She occasionally returned to the stage in the 1950s. Douglas refused to discuss the Senate campaign in later years, although she came out of retirement to campaign for George McGovern in his campaign against Nixon in 1972. She lived in New York City until her death there on June 28, 1980.

FLORENCE PRICE DWYER

United States Representative
Republican of New Jersey
Eighty-fifth–Ninety-second Congresses
January 3, 1957–January 3, 1973

As a Republican representative for sixteen years, Florence Dwyer concentrated on issues of consumer protection, women's equality, and procedural reform in the House of Representatives. Dwyer learned the legislative process on the state level as a lobbyist for the New Jersey Business and Professional Women's Clubs and later as a member of the state assembly from 1950 to 1956, during which time she served as parliamentarian and assistant to the majority leader and speaker.

Dwyer was born Florence Louise Price in Reading, Pennsylvania, on July 4, 1902, and attended school in her hometown. She briefly enrolled at the University of Toledo before marriage and a move to Elizabeth, New

57

Jersey. She first participated in politics as a campaign worker for presidential candidate Wendell Willkie in 1940. Soon thereafter she began her lobbying work in the state capital. In 1950 she was nominated for the state assembly in a crowded primary and won the general election. As a member of the assembly she won passage of a law guaranteeing equal pay for women and established the first minimum salary schedule for teachers throughout New Jersey.

From her success in the assembly she moved on to a race for the House of Representatives from New Jersey's Sixth (later Twelfth) District in 1956 and defeated Democrat Harrison Williams who later served as a U.S. senator. Dwyer served on the Committee on Government Operations throughout her term in the House, and after serving on Veterans' Affair during her freshmen term she joined the Committee on Banking and Currency. On Government Operations she exposed pork-barrel projects, particularly in the area of housing and urban development.

Dwyer was a chief sponsor of the act creating the Consumer Protection Agency and another act that sought to eliminate discriminatory lending practices. She supported the Equal Rights Amendment to the Constitution. In the 1960s Dwyer led a group of Republicans who sought to enlarge the Committee on Rules and thereby diminish the influence of southern Democrats and conservative Republicans who had blocked social and civil rights legislation. During consideration of the Legislative Reorganization Act of 1970, she was author of an amendment requiring the recording of individual teller votes. When her fellow Republican Richard Nixon became president, she urged him to appoint more women to federal office.

Dwyer, who never faced a serious challenge to her seat, decided not to run for reelection in 1972 and retired to Elizabeth, where she died on February 29, 1976.

ELAINE SCHWARTZENBURG EDWARDS

(U.S. House of Representatives)

United States Senator
Democrat of Louisiana
Ninety-second Congress
August 1, 1972–November 13, 1972

Elaine Edwards was appointed to the Senate on August 1, 1972, by her husband, Louisiana Governor Edwin Edwards, to fill the vacancy created by the death of Allen J. Ellender. Governor Edwards' controversial decision to appoint his wife, who made clear her decision not to run for the full Senate term, allowed him to avoid the endorsement of a successor to Ellender, a thirty-five year veteran of the Senate. Elaine Edwards took the oath of office on August 7, 1972, and served on the Committee on Agriculture and Forestry and the Committee on Public Works.

One of Edwards' earliest legislative actions was to join Senator Hubert Humphrey in introducing a bill to establish an educational fellowship in the name of her predecessor. She also co-sponsored an amendment to the Federal Environmental Pesticide Control Act and another to increase the permissible amount of outside income for Social Security recipients. In her first floor speech, Edwards voiced support for a motion calling for a vote on the proposed Equal Education Opportunities Act which would have restricted the use of busing to achieve school integration. Edwards resigned her seat on November 13, 1972, in order that Senator-elect J. Bennett Johnston might gain seniority by finishing the remainder of Ellender's term.

Edwards was born Elaine Lucille Schwartzenburg in Marksville, Louisiana, on March 8, 1929, and she attended local schools.

WILLA McCORD BLAKE ESLICK

(U.S. House of Representatives)

United States Representative
Democrat of Tennessee
Seventy-second Congress
August 4, 1932–March 3, 1933

Willa Eslick sat in the gallery of the House of Representatives on June 14, 1932, as her husband, Representative Edward Everett Eslick fell dead on the chamber floor as he delivered a speech in support of the bonus bill for relief of veterans of the First World War. Less than two months later, on August 4, 1932, Willa Eslick defeated three opponents in the special election to fill her husband's seat from the Seventh District of Tennessee. She was not sworn in until the opening of the second session of the Seventy-second Congress on December 5, 1932. In her brief term she was assigned to the Committee on Public Buildings and Grounds and the Committee on World War Veterans' Legislation.

Eslick devoted most of her time and attention to the plight of farmers, particularly in her largely rural district. She joined seventy-five House Members in an informal group to discuss farm relief and to recommend legislation to alleviate the crisis of agriculture in the Depression. Willa Eslick voted in favor of an emergency farm parity plan proposed by Representative Marvin Jones of Texas, and she supported the Smith bill offering relief to cotton farmers who reduced production. She praised the plans of President-elect Roosevelt to develop the Tennessee River Valley and to construct an electrical-generating plant at Muscle Shoals, Alabama.

Before her election to Congress, Willa Eslick had little political experience beyond service on the state Democratic committee. She was born in Fayetteville, Tennessee, on September 8, 1878, and attended Dick White College, Milton College, the Winthrop Model School and Peabody College before going to New York City where she studied music at the Metropolitan College of Music and the Synthetic School of Music. Because her husband died after the filing deadline for the congressional primary of 1932, Willa Eslick was ineligible for reelection to the Seventy-third Congress. She returned to Tennessee and died in Pulaski on February 18, 1961.

MARY ELIZABETH PRUETT FARRINGTON

(U.S. House of Representatives)

Delegate
Republican of Hawaii
Eighty-third–Eighty-fourth Congresses
July 31, 1954–January 3, 1957

The daughter of missionary parents, Mary Farrington was born in Tokyo on May 30, 1898, and attended Tokyo Foreign School and the grammar schools of Nashville, El Paso, Los Angeles and Hollywood. She graduated from Ward-Belmont Junior College in Nashville in 1916 and from the University of Wisconsin at Madison in 1918. In 1920 she mar-

ried Joseph R. Farrington, son of one of the *Honolulu Star Bulletin's* publishers and a lifelong advocate of Hawaiian statehood who was elected a territorial delegate from Hawaii in 1942.

During the 1920s Mary Farrington founded a Washington-based newspaper syndicate that distributed news items from the capital to periodicals in the Midwest. She served as president of the League of Republican Women in Washington from 1946 to 1948. From 1949 to 1953 she was president of the National Federation of Women's Republican Clubs.

When her husband died on June 19, 1954, Farrington was nominated to succeed him and in the special election held on July 31, 1954, defeated Democrat Delbert Metzger. She ran for a full term in November and narrowly defeated John A. Burns.

Farrington was sworn in as a member of the Eighty-third Congress on August 4, 1954, and served on the Committee on Agriculture, the Committee on Armed Services, and the Committee on Interior and Insular Affairs. She carried on her husband's campaign for Hawaiian statehood and submitted a statehood bill at the opening of the Eighty-fourth Congress in January 1955. She defended Hawaii against charges by anti-statehood forces that communists in general and radical labor leader Harry Bridges in particular held extensive power in the territory.

She ran for reelection in 1956 but lost to Burns whom she beat by only 818 votes in 1954. Farrington resumed her newspaper and broadcasting business and served as president of the *Star Bulletin* from 1957 until 1961. She was also director and chair of the Honolulu Lithograph Company, Ltd., from 1945 to 1963, and president of the Hawaiian Broadcasting System, Ltd., from 1960 to 1963.

In 1969 President Nixon appointed Farrington director of the Office of the Territories in the Department of the Interior. When the Interior Department abolished the post in 1971 she worked in the congressional liaison office until 1973. She returned to Honolulu, where she died on July 21, 1984.

REBECCA LATIMER FELTON

(Georgia Department of Archives and History)

United States Senator
Democrat of Georgia
Sixty-seventh Congress
November 21, 1922–November 22, 1922

Rebecca Felton's brief and essentially symbolic service in the Senate stood in contrast to her decades of substantive participation in Georgia politics and civic affairs. Outspoken, determined, and irascible, Felton was involved in public life from the 1870s through the 1920s. She first entered politics during her husband's successful campaign for the House

of Representatives and went on to a work as a lecturer and newspaper writer, finally becoming the first woman to serve in the United States Senate.

Rebecca Ann Latimer was born on June 10, 1835, near Decatur, De Kalb County, Georgia. She attended several private schools in the area before graduating from Madison Female

College in 1852. The following year she married William H. Felton, an ordained Methodist minister and physician, and lived with him on a farm near Cartersville, Georgia. In the years following the Civil War, the Feltons worked to restore their heavily-damaged farm, and she taught school. In 1874, Rebecca Felton worked as a campaign manager for her husband who ran for Congress on a ticket opposing the "Bourbon" Democrats. She continued to be a close adviser during his three terms in the House and later service in the state legislature.

In conjunction with her husband's political career and in her own work as a lecturer and writer, Rebecca Felton endorsed many of the crusades of Southern progressivism. She supported woman's suffrage, prohibition, and public education, especially vocational training for girls, while fighting the state's system of convict leasing. Felton was also prone to harsh, personal attacks on perceived enemies and articulated an often brutal vision of social order. Even in an age noted for intolerance and racism, Felton's judgements were frequently extreme. She attacked Jews, Catholics, and blacks, going so far as to endorse mass lynchings of blacks as a warning against suspected rapists. Such newspaper columns attracted great attention up through 1920 when she mounted an attack on Woodrow Wilson and the proposed League of Nations in one of her last public campaigns.

Felton's personal determination, if not her varied political views, was much in evidence in her fleeting Senate career. When Senator Tom Watson, an old Populist ally of the Feltons, died in office on September 26, 1922, Governor Thomas Hardwick designated Felton on October 3 as a temporary successor to the Senate seat. The governor, who opposed the Nineteenth Amendment while a member of Congress, hoped the appointment would appease newly enfranchised women, but never intended for the nominee actually to serve before an elected successor could be chosen prior to the reconvening of Congress. The eighty-seven year old Felton, however, convinced Senator-elect Walter George to delay presenting his credentials so that she might be sworn in and serve for two days.

On November 20, 1922, Felton took her seat in the Senate chamber, and the following day she was sworn in as that body's first woman member and the oldest senator at the time of swearing-in. A day later, when the Senate first proceeded to business and beneath a gallery filled with women assembled for the occasion, Felton made brief remarks before resigning her seat in favor of George who was present for the occasion. She thus gained the further and dubious distinction of being the senator with the shortest term of service.

Felton returned to Cartersville, Georgia, and continued to write on public affairs. She died in Atlanta on January 24, 1930.

MILLICENT HAMMOND FENWICK

United States Representatives
Republican of New Jersey
Ninety-fourth–Ninety-seventh Congresses
January 3, 1975–January 3, 1983

Millicent Fenwick, like many women who have served in Congress, entered public affairs as a member of a local school board. Unlike most others, however, Fenwick served on the local board and participated in civic activities while carrying on another career unrelated to politics. After working for Vogue as a model, she served as an associate editor for that magazine and other Condé Nast publications from 1938 to 1952. In 1948 she wrote *Vogue's Book of Etiquette.*

Born Millicent Hammond in New York City on February 25, 1910, she attended Foxcroft School in Virginia until she was fifteen when she accompanied her father as he served as United States ambassador to Spain. Fenwick later attended Columbia University and the New School for Social Research in New York City.

While working in New York, Fenwick served from 1938 to 1947 on the board of education of Bernardsville, New Jersey, where she lived. After retiring from her publication job, she served on the Borough Council from 1958 to 1964 and was a member of the New Jersey Committee of the U.S. Commission on Civil Rights. She entered the state assembly in 1970 and served three years before she became director of New Jersey Consumer Affairs. In 1974 she narrowly defeated fellow Assembly member and future governor, Thomas Kean, for the Republican nomination for the House of Representatives from New Jersey's Fifth District. After winning the general election she gained ever larger majorities in the three succeeding elections.

In her four terms, Fenwick served on a variety of committees and addressed herself to a surprising array of issues. In her first term she was assigned to the Committee on Banking, Currency and Housing and the Committee on Small Business. She also served on the Committee on the District of Columbia, the Committee on Foreign Affairs, the Committee on Education and Labor, and the Select Committee on Aging. Although she was a fiscal conservative, on other matters she differed from many of her Republican colleagues. She supported the Equal Rights Amendment, federal funding for abortions, and the food stamp program. She worked to establish the Helsinki Commission on human rights and worked to eliminate the tax provision that penalized working couples. Fenwick was also interested in procedural reform of the House and served on the Ethics Committee during the investigation of Tongsun Park's attempts to influence Members of Congress.

Fenwick's personal style (she unabashedly smoked a pipe) and her combination of patrician manners, a frank, even blunt, willingness to offer opinions, and political convictions that defied easy categorization gained her a national reputation enjoyed by few four-term Members. She even served as the model for the fictional Congresswoman Lacey Davenport in the "Doonesbury" cartoon series. Fenwick left the House when she was the unsuccessful Republican candidate for the Senate in 1982. From 1983 to 1987 she served as United States representative, with rank of ambassador, to the United Nations Agencies for Food and Agriculture. She is a resident of Bernardsville, New Jersey.

GERALDINE ANNE FERRARO

(U.S. House of Representatives)

United States Representative
Democrat of New York
Ninety-sixth–Ninety-eighth Congresses
January 3, 1979–January 3, 1985

The relatively brief congressional career of Geraldine Ferraro vaulted her into national prominence and provided the foundation for a significant precedent in the history of women's participation in American politics. On July 19, 1984, she became the first woman chosen to run for vice president on the ticket of a major political party when she was nomi-nated by acclamation at the Democratic National Convention.

Ferraro was born in Newburgh, New York, on August 26, 1935. After her father's death eight years later she moved with her mother to the Bronx and afterward to Queens. She graduated from Marymount School in Tarry-town, New York, in 1952 and received a B.A.

from Marymount College in 1956. While attending night classes at Fordham University School of Law in New York City, Ferraro taught in the public schools of Queens. She received her J.D. in 1960 and was admitted to the New York bar in 1961.

Ferraro was appointed an assistant district attorney of Queens County in 1974 and served in that capacity for four years, prosecuting many cases involving rape, child and spouse abuse and domestic violence. When Ninth District Representative James J. Delaney chose not to run for a sixteenth term in 1978, Ferraro won the Democratic nomination to succeed him and captured 54 percent of the vote over the Republican nominee, Alfred A. Delli-Bovi.

Ferraro served on the Committee on Post Office and Civil Service, where she defended the interests of displaced federal workers, and on the Committee on Public Works and Transportation, where she fought for increased federal funds for urban mass transit systems. She centered much of her attention on the issues of wage, pension and retirement account equity for women and was a co-sponsor of the 1981 Economic Equity Act. Ferraro differed from many of her constituents in her pro-choice position on abortion, but she more closely reflected their views with her votes in favor of the Pershing II missile, Trident submarine, an anti-busing amendment to the Constitution, and tuition tax credits.

Upon entering the House of Representatives, Ferraro quickly established a close working relationship with Speaker Thomas P. "Tip" O'Neill, Jr. and other members of the House leadership. During the Ninety-seventh Congress she became secretary of the House Democratic Caucus, which entitled her to a seat on the influential House Steering and Policy Committee. In the Ninety-eighth Congress, Ferraro surrendered her seat on Post Office and Civil Service and accepted appointment to the Budget Committee.

Shortly before the Democratic National Convention convened in San Francisco and following a highly-publicized search process, Ferraro accepted Walter Mondale's offer of nomination for vice president on his presidential ticket. Ferraro's performance as a member of the Hunt Commission to amend the rules used to choose national convention delegates and as chair of the 1984 platform committee had attracted wide praise within the party. Mondale strategists expected her candidacy would convince large numbers of women to vote for a Mondale-Ferraro ticket as well as help win back disaffected Democratic voters in working-class, ethnic neighborhoods of the industrial Northeast. In addition to campaigning in these areas, Ferraro spoke before many women's groups throughout the country and visited college and university campuses, attempting to spark the enthusiasm of young people for the Democratic Party. On October 11 Ferraro met Vice President George Bush in the second nationally televised debate between vice presidential candidates in history. On election day, the Mondale-Ferraro ticket fell far short of victory over Reagan and Bush, receiving 41 percent of the popular vote and carrying the electoral votes of only Minnesota and the District of Columbia.

During 1988 Ferraro was a fellow of the Institute of Politics at Harvard University's John F. Kennedy School of Government. She is currently president of the International Institute for Women's Political Leadership.

BOBBI FIEDLER

United States Representative
Republican of California
Ninety-seventh–Ninety-ninth Congresses
January 3, 1981–January 3, 1987

In her first race for the House of Representatives, Bobbi Fiedler defeated ten-term incumbent and chairman of the Democratic Congressional Campaign Committee, James Corman, in 1980. She began her public career as the organizer of a citizens' group opposed to a busing plan for the desegregation of Los Angeles schools. From her work with BUSTOP in the San Fernando Valley, Fiedler went on to win a seat on the Los Angeles School Board in 1977, and she served on that panel until her campaign for Congress. In her challenge to the incumbent, she emphasized busing, education costs and drug abuse in the schools.

Fiedler was born Roberta Frances Horowitz in Santa Monica, California, on April 22, 1937. After attending public schools, she attended Santa Monica Technical School and Santa Monica City College from 1955 to 1959. She worked in the pharmacy business and as an interior decorator before entering public life.

Fiedler's victory over Democrat James Corman rested on fewer than 800 votes on an election day when President Jimmy Carter conceded his own defeat three hours before the polls closed in California. While the Reagan landslide may have carried her into office, Fiedler had no trouble winning reelection to her Twenty-first District seat, particularly after the boundaries were redrawn to include much of the district represented by Barry Goldwater, Jr. before his unsuccessful Senate bid.

In her three House terms, Fiedler sat on the Budget Committee where she was an advocate of fiscal conservatism. Although she was a strong supporter of the Reagan administration on most issues, she broke with some of her Republican colleagues in her support of the Equal Rights Amendment and other feminist issues. In 1986 Fiedler unsuccessfully ran in the Republican primary for the Republican nomination to the Senate rather than run for reelection. She is a resident of Northridge, California.

WILLA LYBRAND FULMER

United States Representative
Democrat of South Carolina
Seventy-eighth Congress
November 7, 1944–January 3, 1945

Willa Fulmer accepted nomination to fill the vacancy in South Carolina's Second District left by the death of her husband, Hampton Pitts Fulmer, with no intention of running in the concurrent election for the following Congress. Shortly after Hampton Fulmer's death on October 19, 1944, the South Carolina Democratic executive committee asked his widow to run for the short-term vacancy. On November 7, Wilma Fulmer was elected without opposition to fill out the remaining weeks in the term of her husband, a veteran of more than twenty-three years House service and the chairman of the Committee on Agriculture. She was sworn in on November 16, 1944, and Congress adjourned a month later without her receiving a committee assignment.

Willa Lybrand was born February 3, 1884, in Wagener, South Carolina. She attended public schools in her hometown and the Greenville Female Seminary before her marriage to Fulmer. She died at sea, while sailing to Europe, on May 13, 1968.

ELIZABETH HAWLEY GASQUE

(U.S. House of Representatives)

United States Representative
Democrat of South Carolina
Seventy-fifth Congress
September 13, 1938–January 3, 1939

As the lone candidate in the special election of September 13, 1938, Elizabeth Gasque succeeded her late husband in little more than name. The Seventy-fifth Congress adjourned before she was elected as representative from South Carolina's Sixth District which her husband, Allard H. Gasque, had represented from 1923 until his death in June 1938. She was never sworn into office and was not a candidate for reelection.

Elizabeth Mills Hawley was born on Rice Creek Plantation near Blythewood, South Carolina, on February 26, 1896. She attended the South Carolina Coeducational Institute in Edgefield and graduated with a degree in expression from Greenville Female College in

1907. After the death of her husband and her brief service, she returned to live in South Carolina and later married A.J. Van Exem, but maintained her social ties in Washington. She died on November 2, 1989.

FLORENCE REVILLE GIBBS

(U.S. House of Representatives)

United States Representative
Democrat of Georgia
Seventy-sixth Congress
October 1, 1940–January 3, 1941

Florence Gibbs entered Congress to serve out the final three months in the term of her husband, Willis B. Gibbs, who died in his freshman term in the House of Representatives. She won the uncontested special election for Georgia's Eighth Congressional District on October 1, 1940, in a predictably low turnout of voters. She took the oath of office on October 3, and served until January 3, 1941, without a committee assignment.

Gibbs, who had no public career prior or subsequent to her service in the House, was born Florence Reville in Thomson, Georgia, on April 4, 1890, and graduated from Brenau College in Gainesville, Georgia. After retiring from her brief term in Congress, she returned to Jesup, Georgia, where she died on August 19, 1964.

KATHRYN ELIZABETH GRANAHAN

(U.S. House of Representatives)

United States Representative
Democrat of Pennsylvania
Eighty-fourth–Eighty-seventh Congresses
November 6, 1956–January 3, 1963

Kathryn Granahan, known to many Americans from her signature on currency while Treasurer of the United States, gained attention in Congress as the leader of an investigation of pornography and its effects on minors. She was born Kathryn Elizabeth O'Hay in Easton, Pennsylvania, on December 7, 1894, and was educated in the public schools of Easton and Mount St. Joseph Collegiate Institute in Philadelphia.

From 1940 to 1943 O'Hay was supervisor of public assistance in the state auditor general's department, and liaison officer between that department and Pennsylvania's Department of Public Assistance. In 1943 she married William T. Granahan, Democratic leader of

Philadelphia's Fifty-second Ward and chief disbursing officer for the Pennsylvania treasury, who was elected in 1944 to represent Pennsylvania's Second District in the House of Representatives. He lost his bid for reelection in the national Republican sweep of 1946, but was returned to office in 1948. William Granahan was renominated for a fifth term in the April 1956 primary, but he died on May 25.

Following her husband's death, Kathryn Granahan succeeded him as leader of the Fifty-second Ward, and on June 11 she was nominated to replace her husband as the Democratic candidate for the Eighty-fourth Congress. She defeated Robert F. Frankenfield on November 6, 1956, and was elected at the same time to a full term in the Eighty-fifth Congress.

Granahan served on the Committee on the District of Columbia, the Committee on Government Operations, and the Committee on Post Office and Civil Service. She generally supported the Democratic leadership and voted for the Civil Rights Act of 1957, a housing bill for veterans, an increase in the wages of federal employees and increased financial support for federal regulatory agencies. In May 1959, as chair of the Post Office and Civil Service subcommittee on postal operations, she called on private citizens and organizations to help take the lead in crushing the pornography trade. In August she introduced legislation requiring mandatory jail sentences for persons found guilty of operating pornographic mail order businesses. Granahan was a chief sponsor of a bill passed by the House in September 1959 that strengthened the Post Office's power to impound mail addressed to recipients suspected of mailing pornographic materials. In 1961 she counseled the Supreme Court to issue stricter guidelines to help authorities determine if publications were obscene. When the census of 1960 revealed that Philadelphia would lose one of its six House seats, Democratic City Committee chair and Fifth District Representative William J. Green, Jr., selected Granahan's seat for elimination. Green and other Democratic leaders convinced President Kennedy to appoint her Treasurer of the United States as recompense.

Granahan took the oath of office as Treasurer on January 9, 1963. In January 1964 she proposed the return of the two-dollar bill to circulation. In May 1965 Granahan left work following brain surgery necessitated by a fall. In June 1966 a Philadelphia Orphans Court judge set aside a petition to have her declared incompetent and to appoint a guardian to her estate. On October 13 she submitted her resignation to Treasury Secretary Henry H. Fowler.

Granahan died in Norristown, Pennsylvania, on July 10, 1979.

ELLA TAMBUSSI GRASSO

United States Representative
Democrat of Connecticut
Ninety-second–Ninety-third Congresses
January 3, 1971–January 3, 1975

Ella Grasso's two terms in the House of Representatives were a small part of an extended political career that culminated when she became the first woman elected as a state governor in her own right. Most of her public life was devoted to the state politics of her native Connecticut where she served in the state assembly and as secretary of state before her election as chief executive. Her rise to political power followed the traditional pattern of Democratic politics in a northeastern state.

Grasso was born Ella Rosa Giovanna Oliva Tambussi in Windsor Locks, Connecticut, on May 10, 1919. Her parents were Italian immigrants who provided her with a modest if comfortable upbringing. As the recipient of various scholarships, however, Grasso enjoyed the finest of educational opportunities. She graduated from the Chaffee School in her hometown and was elected to Phi Beta Kappa at Mount Holyoke College where she graduated with a B.A. in 1940 and received her M.A. two years later. During the Second World War Grasso worked as a researcher for the War Manpower Commission and first became involved in politics as a member of the League of Women Voters.

As the veteran of local campaign organizations and as a protege of Connecticut's legendary Democratic leader, John Bailey, Grasso entered electoral politics in 1952 when she won a seat in the state house of representatives. In her second term she became assistant Democratic leader of the state legislature. In the unlikely post of secretary of state for Connecticut from 1958 to 1970 Grasso became one of the best-known and most popular political figures in the state through her personal attention to citizens' concerns and her public ceremonial duties. At the same time, she continued to be active in Democratic party affairs and at the Democratic National Convention at Chicago in 1968 proposed a platform plank condemning the United States involvement in the Vietnam War.

In 1970 Grasso entered the race for the empty House seat from Connecticut's Sixth District. In her campaign she again called for withdrawal of American troops from Vietnam and concentrated on the economic needs of her district where unemployment was a chronic problem. After a close victory, Grasso served as a member of the Committee on Education and Labor and the Committee on Veterans' Affairs where she sponsored a variety of legislation designed to increase employment and protect workers. One of the most important accomplishments of her two terms was her part in drafting the Comprehensive Employment and Training Act. The work of Capitol Hill, however, never engaged Grasso the way Connecticut politics had. Early in her second term, her name was mentioned as a possible candidate for governor, and in January 1974 she announced her intention to run for that office.

Grasso defeated her House colleague, Representative Robert Steele, to win the gubernatorial race and become the first woman in the nation to do so. The election attracted nationwide attention despite Grasso's attempts to downplay the significance of her gender and her lack of involvement with the feminist movement. The fiscal problems of Connecticut forced Grasso to follow a far more conservative policy as governor than she had as a Member of Congress. In her efforts to reduce state spending she started with the symbolic action of returning a pay raise for herself and then imposed a variety of spending cuts to avoid the imposition of an income tax. Grasso also increased the authority of the Department of Public Utilities Control in an effort to restrict the rise in utility rates.

Grasso maintained her popularity despite her reduction in state spending and she won reelection in 1978. In 1979 she was elected chair of the Democratic Governors' Conference. Grasso resigned as governor due to illness on December 31, 1980, and she died in Hartford on February 5, 1981.

DIXIE BIBB GRAVES

(Alabama Department of Archives and History)

United States Senator
Democrat of Alabama
Seventy-fifth Congress
August 20, 1937–January 10, 1938

Governor Bibb Graves of Alabama provoked a storm of criticism in 1937 when he named his wife, Dixie Bibb Graves, to fill the Senate seat vacated by Hugo Black who resigned to accept his nomination as associate justice of the U.S. Supreme Court. By avoiding the endorsement of intra-party rivals for Black's seat, Governor Graves maintained his political allies at the same time that he subjected himself to charges of nepotism and a disregard for the needs of constituents.

For her part, Dixie Bibb Graves found celebrity and condemnation for her speech on the Senate floor on November 19, 1937, during debate on the Wagner-Van Nuys Anti-Lynching Bill. Federal enforcement of an anti-lynching law, she maintained, was a dangerous infringement of state sovereignty and an insult to the law enforcement officers of the South whom she thought responsible for a decrease in lynching over the previous decade. Without federal interference, lynching might be eliminated in five years, according to Graves. While northern newspapers denounced Graves' remarks, Governor Graves distributed copies of the speech throughout Alabama, and white citizens mounted a write-in campaign to place Dixie Graves' name in the special election for the remainder of Black's term.

Graves declined to run in the special election which was won by Representative Lister Hill when he defeated former Senator J. Thomas Heflin. On January 10, 1938, six days after the special election, Graves resigned from the Senate in order that her husband might appoint Hill to the seat immediately. During her five months in office she served on the Committee on Claims, the Committee on Education and Labor, and the Committee on Mines and Mining.

Dixie Bibb was born July 26, 1882, on a plantation at Hope Hull, Alabama, near Montgomery, where she was raised with her orphaned cousin, Bibb Graves. The two married in 1900. She was involved in a wide variety of civic organizations and clubs such as the Women's Christian Temperance Union and the Alabama Federation of Women's Clubs. From 1915 to 1917 she was president of the United Daughters of the Confederacy. Graves died in Montgomery, Alabama, on January 21, 1965.

EDITH STARRETT GREEN

United States Representative
Democrat of Oregon
Eighty-fourth–Ninety-third Congresses
January 3, 1955–December 31, 1974

Few women in Congress have left such a substantial legacy as did Edith Green, and few have demonstrated such independence of mind and deed. She left her mark on almost every education bill enacted during her tenure and gained considerable influence in the Democratic Party despite her refusal to support the party's presidents on all issues.

Green supported federal aid to education and the anti-poverty programs of the Great Society at the same time that she resisted the expansion of the federal bureaucracy.

Edith Starrett was born in Trent, South Dakota, on January 17, 1910, and moved with her family to Oregon six years later. She attended schools in Salem, Oregon, and Willamette University before graduating with a B.S. from the University of Oregon in 1939. She began to teach in 1930 and in the 1940s worked as a radio announcer in Portland. She also pursued graduate courses at Stanford University.

Green's first involvement with public life came through her interest in education and as a local participant in Democratic party affairs. She served as legislative chairman of the Oregon Congress of Parents and Teachers and directed several statewide educational conferences. After an unsuccessful campaign for secretary of state of Oregon in 1952, she entered the race for the House seat from Oregon's Third District in 1954 and defeated Republican Tom McCall, a future governor who had defeated the incumbent in the Republican primary. Green, who emphasized educational issues in her campaign and was already a recognized expert on education policy, was appointed to the Committee on Education and Labor in her freshman term in the House of Representatives. She served on that committee until her final term in Congress when she took a seat on the Committee on Appropriations. Green also served various terms on other House committees including Interior and Insular Affairs, House Administration, Merchant Marine and Fisheries, and District of Columbia.

Green played a central role in the enactment of the National Defense Education Act that passed in 1958 in the wake of public concern about the Soviet success with the Sputnik satellite. She was the author of the Higher Education Facilities Act of 1963 and the Higher Education Act of 1965. As chair of the Education and Labor subcommittee on higher education, she was responsible for establishing the first federal program for undergraduate scholarships.

At the Democratic National Convention in 1956, Green seconded the presidential nomination of Adlai Stevenson and four years later gave a seconding speech for John F. Kennedy. She had managed Kennedy's surprise victory in the Oregon primary that year. After his inauguration, Kennedy offered Green the position of ambassador to Canada, which she declined, and appointed her to the Presidential Committee on the Status of Women. One of Green's perennial concerns was equal pay for men and women in similar government jobs.

Although she supported much of his Great Society program and worked behind the scenes to secure passage of Lyndon Johnson's anti-poverty legislation, she incurred the president's disapproval in 1965 when she was one of only six House Members to vote against his request for increased funds for the escalation of military involvement in Vietnam.

In the 1970s Green's longstanding mistrust of big government brought her to reject much of the social legislation she had worked for in the 1950s and 1960s. She feared that welfare programs had done little to alleviate the problem and wanted states to assume more responsibility for education programs. Her drift from the Democratic party accelerated and in 1976, after having left the House, she was a co-chair of Democrats for Gerald Ford.

Although virtually assured of reelection for the indefinite future, Green did not run in 1974. In retirement she taught at Warner Pacific College and in 1979 was appointed to the Oregon Board of Higher Education. She died in Tulatin, Oregon, on April 21, 1987.

ISABELLA SELMES GREENWAY

United States Representative
Democrat of Arizona
Seventy-third–Seventy-fourth Congresses
October 3, 1933–January 3, 1937

Arizona's only woman representative and one of its leading citizens from the time of statehood through the 1950s, Isabella Greenway entered politics as a supporter of her close personal friend, Franklin Roosevelt. She was born Isabella Selmes on March 22, 1886, in Boone County, Kentucky. She attended public schools in St. Paul, Minnesota, and Miss Chapin's School in New York City, where she began a lifelong friendship with Eleanor Roosevelt. While serving as a bridesmaid at Eleanor Roosevelt's wedding, Selmes met Robert M. Ferguson, a former Rough Rider, whom she married in 1905. To revive his failing health they moved to the southwest in 1909 and homesteaded near Silver

City, New Mexico. In 1918 Isabella Ferguson served as chair of the Women's Land Army of New Mexico. After Robert Ferguson's death in 1922 she moved to Santa Barbara, California, and later accompanied her second husband, a mining engineer and also a former Rough Rider, John C. Greenway, to Ajo, Arizona. Following his death she moved to Tucson, Arizona, and in 1929 established the Arizona Inn, a hotel resort, and a factory where disabled veterans made and sold furniture and household decorations. She also owned and operated a cattle ranch and a Los Angeles-based airline.

In 1928 Greenway used her election as Democratic National committeewoman, widely regarded as a tribute to her late husband, as an opportunity to initiate a serious political career of her own. She traveled extensively throughout the state on behalf of Democratic candidates. In 1932 she worked to swing Arizona's delegation behind the presidential candidacy of Franklin Roosevelt and seconded his nomination before the Democratic National Convention. After Arizona's at-large representative, Lewis W. Douglas, resigned in March 1933 to become director of the Bureau of the Budget, Greenway ran for his seat in an October special election and won an overwhelming victory over Republican and Socialist candidates.

During the Seventy-fourth Congress Greenway served on the Committee on Indian Affairs, the Committee on Irrigation and Reclamation, and the Committee on Public Lands. Soon after winning office, she secured from Secretary of the Interior Harold Ickes a large Public Works Administration project for Arizona. In June 1934 she offered a bill to amend the Cotton Control Act (Bankhead Act), which had established national quotas to regulate cotton production. She submitted measures to transfer Veterans' Administration lands to the Interior Department for the benefit of Yavapai Indians, protect land resources against soil erosion, and improve public grazing lands. She also proposed resolutions to use relief funds to construct homes for elderly public pensioners and to increase employment in the District of Columbia.

Greenway continued her activities on behalf of veterans by introducing legislation to build additions to Veterans' Administration facilities in Tucson and Whipple, Arizona, and to assist veterans who settled on homesteads. Although she was sometimes accused of receiving undue benefits because of her friendship with the First Family, she broke with the Roosevelt administration over the Economy Act of 1933, which cut veterans' pensions.

In March 1936 Greenway announced that she would not be a candidate for renomination in order to devote more time to her family and her business interests. Three years later she married Harry O. King. Opposed to a third presidential term for Roosevelt, she chaired the Arizona chapter of Democrats for Willkie in 1940. She was national chair of the American Women's Volunteer Service during the Second World War. Greenway was also active in international cultural exchange programs before her death in Tucson on December 18, 1953.

MARTHA WRIGHT GRIFFITHS

(U.S. House of Representatives)

United States Representative
Democrat of Michigan
Eighty-fourth–Ninety-third Congresses
January 3, 1955–December 31, 1974

Martha Griffiths, perhaps best known for her promotion of the Equal Rights Amendment, was an advocate of tax, welfare and health care reform throughout her two decades in Congress. She was born Martha Edna Wright in Pierce City, Missouri, on January 29, 1912, and attended the public schools in her hometown. She received a B.A. from the University of Missouri at Columbia in 1934 and accompanied her new husband, Hicks G. Griffiths, to the University of Michigan Law School where she received a J.D. in 1940. She was admitted to the bar in 1941 and entered the legal department of the American Automobile Insurance Company.

In 1942 Griffiths became a contract negotiator for the United States Army in the Detroit Ordnance District and served until she entered private practice in Detroit with her husband in April 1946. Later that year she made her first bid for elective office in an unsuccessful campaign for a seat in the Michigan House of Representatives from Wayne County. Griffiths was elected to the first of two terms in the legislature in 1948, the same year she and her husband joined other reformers to organize the Michigan Democratic Club, which helped engineer the election of G. Mennen Williams as governor. Williams appointed her in April 1953 to fill an unexpired term as recorder and judge of Recorders Court in Detroit. Seven months later she was elected judge and served until 1954.

Griffiths was the Democratic nominee for Congress in the election of 1952 in Michigan's Seventeenth District, but she lost to Republican Charles G. Oakman. Two years later, after campaigning out of a house trailer and travelling extensively through the district, she defeated Oakman to win election to the Eighty-fourth Congress.

Griffiths was a member of the Committee on Banking and Currency, the Committee on Government Operations, and the Joint Economic Committee from the Eighty-seventh through the Ninety-third Congresses. During the Ninety-first Congress she served on the Select Committee on Crime. Early in her House career Griffiths supported urban renewal and food stamp programs and increased federal aid for education and hospital construction. She sponsored legislation to raise the salaries of postal employees and to televise House proceedings. In a move that astonished many observers, she ran for her former position as judge of the Detroit Recorders Court but was defeated in the April 1959 election.

In 1962 Griffiths became the first woman representative to win appointment to the Committee on Ways and Means. From that committee she pursued tax reform and proposed legislation to repeal the excise tax on automobiles, provide tax relief for single parents, and reduce social security taxes paid by low-income families. By the time of her retirement she was the Committee's fourth-ranking member.

In 1970 Griffiths joined Massachusetts Senator Edward M. Kennedy in sponsoring the Health Security Act to institute a national health insurance program financed through payroll, self-employment and unearned income taxes as well as federal revenue.She chaired the Joint Economic Committee's Fiscal Policy Subcommittee, which embarked in 1971 on a three-year study of the nation's welfare system. The study's findings led Griffiths to introduce the 1974 Tax Credits and Allowances Act, designed to reorganize and improve national public assistance programs by providing per capita tax credits for moderate and low-income families and uniform allowances for basic living expenses.

Deeply committed to women's rights, Griffiths helped frame the sex discrimination amendment to Title VII of the 1964 Civil Rights Act and prompted the Equal Employment Opportunity Commission to enforce the act more vigorously. In August 1970 she gathered the necessary signatures on a discharge petition that brought the proposed Equal Rights Amendment out of the Judiciary Committee, where Chairman Emanuel Celler had withheld passage, and on to overwhelming approval on the House floor.

Griffiths declined to be a candidate in 1974 for renomination to an eleventh term. In 1982 she returned to politics as Michigan's first elected lieutenant governor on a ticket with Eighteenth District Representative James J. Blanchard. She and Governor Blanchard were reelected in 1986. On August 24, 1990, Blanchard announced that Griffiths would not be retained as his running mate for a third term. She is a resident of Detroit, Michigan.

KATIE BEATRICE HALL

(Congressional Black Caucus)

United States Representative
Democrat of Indiana
Ninety-seventh–Ninety-eighth Congresses
November 2, 1982–January 3, 1985

In July 1983, during her only full term in the House of Representatives, Katie Hall introduced the bill to make the birthday of Martin Luther King, Jr., a federal holiday. The bill was signed into law in November of the same year. In addition to this commemorative act, Hall devoted much of her attention to the economic problems of her urban and industrial district in northwest Indiana.

Hall was born Katie Beatrice Green in Mound Bayou, Mississippi, on April 3, 1938. She attended school in her hometown and graduated with a B.S. from Mississippi Valley State University in 1960. In 1968 she received her M.S. from Indiana University. Following

91

her graduation from college she taught social studies in the schools of Gary, Indiana. She became involved in politics through the mayoral campaigns of Richard Hatcher of Gary. By 1974 she entered electoral politics herself and became a member of the Indiana House of Representatives. Two years later she was elected to the Indiana Senate and served until 1982. She was chair of the Lake County Democratic Committee from 1978 to 1980.

In September 1982, the chair of Indiana's First District Democratic committee nominated Hall to run for the vacancy left by the death of Representative Adam Benjamin, Jr., and for the full term in the Ninety-eighth Congress. In the election of November 2, Hall defeated Republican Thomas Krieger to win the First District seat for the remainder of the Ninety-seventh Congress and for the succeeding term. As a Member of the House of Representatives she served on the Committee on Post Office and Civil Service and the Committee on Public Works and Transportation.

Hall supported a variety of legislation designed to alleviate her district's high rate of unemployment and attendant social ramifications. She endorsed the Fair Trade in Steel Act which was intended to revitalize the steel industry. She supported the Humphrey-Hawkins bill for full employment and measures to prevent child abuse and family violence. Hall also endorsed the Equal Rights Amendment to the Constitution.

In her bid for renomination in 1984, Hall lost the Democratic primary to Peter Visclosky. She continued to be active in Democratic politics and served as a state senator from Indiana's third district. In 1986 and again in 1990 she failed in her bid to win nomination to the House of Representatives. She is a resident of Gary, Indiana.

JULIA BUTLER HANSEN

(U.S. House of Representatives)

United States Representative
Democrat of Washington
Eighty-sixth–Ninety-third Congresses
November 8, 1960–December 31, 1974

Julia Butler Hansen's seven terms in the House capped a career of forty-three years in elective office on the municipal, state and federal levels. She was born Julia Caroline Butler on June 14, 1907, in Portland, Oregon. After attending the public schools of Washington and Oregon State College from 1924 to 1926 she worked her way through the University of Washington at Seattle as a dietician and swimming instructor and received a degree in home economics in 1930.

In 1938 Hansen was elected to the Cathlamet, Washington, city council and served until 1946. She was a member of the state house of representatives from January 1939 until her election to Congress, serving as speaker pro tempore from 1955 to 1960 and developing an expertise on transportation issues. She also chaired the Eleven Western States Highway Policy Committee from 1951 to 1960 and managed a title and casualty insurance business from 1958 to 1961.

Following the death of Third District Representative Russell V. Mack on March 28, 1960, Hansen entered the race to succeed him and was elected to fill the vacancy in the Eighty-sixth Congress. At the same time she was elected to the Eighty-seventh Congress.

Hansen served briefly on the Committee on Veterans' Affairs during the first session of the Eighty-seventh Congress and was a member of the Committee on Education and Labor and the Committee of Interior and Insular Affairs during the Eighty-seventh Congress. As a member of the Committee on Appropriations from 1963 to 1974, she chaired its Subcommittee on Interior and Related Agencies.

Hansen introduced joint resolutions calling for establishment of a national traffic safety agency and an independent Federal Maritime Administration. She proposed construction of a Veterans' Administration hospital in Vancouver, Washington, the regulation of dairy imports, and a joint Congressional committee to investigate crime. In October 1967 she offered a concurrent resolution in support of United Nations peace keeping forces and urged President Johnson to seek U.N. meditation for the war in Vietnam.

During her final term Hansen chaired the Democratic Committee on Organization, Study and Review, which recommended the first changes in committee structure since passage of the Legislative Reorganization Act of 1946. An amended version of the Hansen plan, approved by the House in October 1974, included provisions to expand permanent committee staff, prohibit voting by proxy in committee, require committees of more than fifteen members to have at least four subcommittees and require the House to meet in December of election years to organize itself for the next Congress.

Hansen announced in February 1974 that she would not run for renomination to an eighth term and resigned her seat on the last day of the year. In 1975 she was appointed to a six-year term on the Washington State Toll Bridge Authority and State Highway Commission, which she had helped create during her years in the legislature. She also chaired the Washington State Transportation Commission from 1979 until her resignation in 1980. She resided in Cathlamet until her death there on May 3, 1988.

CECIL MURRAY HARDEN

(U.S. House of Representatives)

United States Representative
Republican of Indiana
Eighty-first–Eighty-fifth Congresses
January 3, 1949–January 3, 1959

Cecil Harden, whose interest in politics was awakened by meetings of the local Republican Party in a room above her husband's automobile dealership, eventually won five terms in the House of Representatives. She was born in Covington, Indiana, on November 21, 1894, graduated from its public schools in 1912, and attended the University of Indiana at Bloom-

ington. Beginning in 1912 she taught in the Troy Township schools of Fountain County, Indiana, and in the public schools of Covington before her marriage to Frost R. Harden in December 1914.

When her husband lost his presidential appointment as Covington's postmaster following the Democratic victory of 1932, Harden became active in Republican politics, serving as vice-chair of a precinct committee. She chaired the Fountain County Republican Party from 1938 until 1950 and served as Republican national committeewoman from Indiana from 1944 to 1959 and from 1964 until 1972. She was an at-large delegate to the Republican national conventions of 1948, 1952, 1956 and 1968.

After Representative Noble J. Johnson resigned his Sixth District seat in July 1948 to accept a federal customs and patent appeals court judgeship, Harden was chosen to be the Republican nominee and defeated the Democratic nominee, Jack O'Grady, by only 483 votes out of over 132,000 cast. She was appointed to the Committee on Veterans' Affairs in her freshman term, transferred to the Committee on Expenditures in Executive Departments in the following term, and served on the Committee on Government Operations and the Committee on Post Office and Civil Service in the Eighty-third through Eighty-fifth Congresses.

Like Virginia Jenckes, who had represented much of the same district during the 1930s,

Harden promoted flood control for the Wabash Valley and secured funding for a dam and recreational facility. She criticized the Defense Department's 1956 plans to close the Atomic Energy Commission's heavy water plant in Dana, Indiana, claiming that the closing would put nine hundred people out of work and add to her district's already severe unemployment problems. As a member of the Committee on Expenditures in Executive Departments, she toured military supply installations in the United States and Asia to study ways of improving the armed forces' procurement procedures.

Harden was defeated by Fred Wampler in her bid for reelection to a sixth term in 1958, one of five Indiana Republicans who lost seats in a national Democratic sweep which cost the GOP forty-seven House seats. Two months after leaving Congress, Harden was appointed special assistant for women's affairs to Postmaster General Arthur E. Summerfield and served until March 1961. In August 1970 she was appointed to the National Advisory Committee for the White House Conference on Aging. She died in Lafayette, Indiana, on December 5, 1984.

PAULA FICKES HAWKINS

(U.S. Senate Historical Office)

United States Senator
Republican of Florida
January 1, 1981–January 3, 1987

In a familiar path for women in politics, Paula Hawkins first entered public affairs as a community activist and volunteer for the local political party organization. From her work with parents' organizations and as the leader of a neighborhood effort to improve public utilities, Hawkins won statewide election to the Florida Public Service Commission and from there mounted campaigns for congressional office. At the same time she served in various capacities with the local Republican Party and developed ties with Republican leaders from throughout the state.

Hawkins was born Paula Fickes in Salt Lake City, Utah, on January 24, 1927, and as a young girl lived in various places as the daughter of a navy chief warrant officer. She attended schools in Atlanta and graduated from high school in Logan, Utah. She attended Utah State University for several years and enrolled in secretarial courses before getting her first job as a secretary at Utah State. Following her marriage she moved to Atlanta and in 1955 to central Florida.

In the 1960s Hawkins won a succession of positions with the Republican Party that carried her into the world of state politics. After organizing Edward Gurney's successful House campaign in 1966 and serving as a Florida co-chair of Nixon's presidential campaigns in 1968 and 1972, Hawkins won her first elective office in 1972 when she gained a seat on the state Public Services Commission. In her two terms with that body she earned a reputation as a consumer-rights advocate and opponent of rate increases by utility companies. Hawkins resigned from the commission in 1979 to become vice president for consumer affairs for Air Florida.

While serving on the Public Services Commission, Hawkins sought election as United States senator in 1974 and as lieutenant governor in 1976. In 1980 she again entered the campaign for the Senate in a crowded Republican primary with few divisive issues. After failing to win a majority, Hawkins gained the nomination in a runoff and faced former Representative William Gunter in the general election. She narrowly won the seat in an election year when Ronald Reagan swept Florida in the presidential contest and Republicans gained control of the Senate.

Hawkins served on the Committee on Agriculture, Nutrition, and Forestry and the Committee on Labor and Human Resources throughout her Senate term and in the Ninety-eighth Congress also served on the Committee on Banking, Housing, and Urban Affairs and the Committee on Foreign Relations. She was a member of the Joint Economic Committee in the Ninety-seventh Congress and the Special Committee on Aging in the Ninety-ninth Congress.

In her second year in the Senate, Hawkins focused on an issue that became the centerpiece of her legislative attention for the remainder of her term. She initiated a year-long investigation of the problem of missing children, one result of which was the Missing Children's Act of 1982 which provided for a central information center for missing children. Hawkins sponsored other legislation to facilitate the search for children and to provide federal guidelines for the prevention of abuse in child-care centers and institutions. Hawkins gained attention for the issue with a dramatic revelation of her own abuse as a child.

Hawkins was generally supportive of the Reagan administration in foreign policy and economic matters. She opposed funding for abortion and the Equal Rights Amendment. She favored increased federal spending in various programs dealing with the elderly.

In 1986, when Democrats regained a majority in the Senate, Hawkins was unable to hold her seat against the challenge from Florida governor Bob Graham. She is a resident of Winter Park, Florida.

MARGARET M. HECKLER

(U.S. House of Representatives)

United States Representative
Republican of Massachusetts
Ninetieth–Ninety-seventh Congresses
January 3, 1967–January 3, 1983

On September 13, 1966, Margaret Heckler brought one of the legendary careers of Massachusetts politics to an end when she defeated Representative Joseph W. Martin for the Republican nomination to represent the Tenth District. At eighty-one, Martin had been a member of Congress since 1925 and had served as House Republican leader for sixteen years and as Speaker for four.

Heckler was born Margaret Mary O'Shaughnessy on June 21, 1931, in Flushing, New York. She studied at the University of Leiden, The Netherlands in 1952 and received a B.A. from Albertus Magnus College in 1953. She received an LL.B. in 1956 from Boston

College Law School where she was editor of the law review. From 1958 until her election to Congress she was a member of the Republican town committee of Wellesley, Massachusetts, and volunteered to work for the campaigns of local GOP candidates. In 1962 Heckler won a seat on the Massachusetts Governor's Council and was reelected in 1964.

In her campaign against the venerable Martin, Heckler reminded voters that he had first won his House seat from an eighty-three year-old incumbent, William S. Greene, by convincing the district it needed more vigorous service in Washington. Following her primary victory, Heckler won the general election over the Democratic candidate, Patrick H. Harrington, Jr.

Like another Republican Representative from Massachusetts, Edith Nourse Rogers, Heckler devoted much of her attention to the problems and needs of veterans and eventually became the second-ranking Republican member of the Veterans' Affairs Committee. She favored installation of aging centers in Veterans' Administration hospitals and the creation of counseling facilities for veterans of the Vietnam War. An advocate of child care for working parents, she criticized President Nixon's December 1971 veto of a comprehensive child development program.

In addition to her service on Veterans' Affairs for the full span of her years in Congress, Heckler served on the Committee on Government Operations in the Ninetieth Congress, on Banking and Currency in the Ninety-first through Ninety-third Congresses, on Agriculture in the Ninety-fourth through Ninety-sixth Congresses, on Science and Technology in the Ninety-seventh Congress, and on the Select Committee on Ethics in the Ninety-sixth Congress. She was also a member of the Joint Economic Committee in the Ninety-fourth, Ninety-sixth and Ninety-seventh Congresses.

Heckler supported the proposed Equal Rights Amendment to the Constitution and co-sponsored an October 1977 joint resolution to extend the deadline for its ratification. She also drafted the Equal Credit Opportunity Act of 1974 and joined Representative Elizabeth Holtzman of New York to organize the Congressional Caucus for Women's Issues in 1977. Heckler opposed the use of federal funds for abortions and endorsed tuition tax credits for parents with children in private, non-profit schools.

By 1982, redistricting removed Heckler's Tenth District from the electoral map and pitted her against the Fourth District's Representative Barney Frank. Heckler lost the spirited campaign in which Frank concentrated on her support for President Reagan's budget and economic plan of 1981.

On January 12, 1983, Reagan nominated Heckler as Secretary of the Department of Health and Human Services. She was confirmed by the Senate on March 3. As secretary, Heckler managed the establishment of new guidelines for the Social Security disability program and led a campaign to increase federal funding for research and care for patients with Alzheimer's Disease and AIDS.

In December 1985 Reagan named Heckler Ambassador to Ireland, and she served in that position until October 1989. She is a resident of Wellesley, Massachusetts.

LOUISE DAY HICKS

(U.S. House of Representatives)

United States Representative
Democrat of Massachusetts
Ninety-second Congress
January 3, 1971–January 3, 1973

In her single term in the House of Representatives, Louise Day Hicks achieved none of the notoriety that she gained when she served in local offices in her native Boston. As a member of the Boston School Committee and the Boston City Council, Hicks gained national attention for her efforts to block school integration plans that depended upon the busing of students. While she served in Congress, much of her attention remained focused on Boston where she entered her second mayoral race during her first session in Washington.

Anna Louise Day was born in Boston on October 16, 1923, the daughter of a Democratic district court judge. She graduated from

Wheelock Teachers' College in 1938 and received her B.S. from Boston University School of Education in 1955. In 1958 Hicks graduated with a J.D. from Boston University School of Law. She formed a law partnership with her brother in Boston.

Hicks was elected to the Boston School Committee in 1961 and served most of her initial two-year term with little controversy. Beginning in 1963, however, she emerged as the leading defender of "neighborhood schools" against the NAACP and other groups seeking the racial integration of Boston schools. She was reelected with nearly three-quarters of the vote in 1963 and as chairman of the school committee in 1965 faced a Massachusetts law that required local jurisdictions to implement desegregation plans or lose state funds. Hicks nevertheless rejected a busing plan for Boston. Although she lost the election for state treasurer in 1964, she easily won a third term to the school committee the following year and in 1967 entered the mayoral race on the slogan "You know where I stand." She lost the campaign to Kevin White.

Hicks returned to political office in 1969 when she was elected to the Boston City Council. When Ninth District Representative (and Speaker of the House) John McCormack announced his retirement in 1970, Hicks won his seat in a campaign that emphasized law and order. In the Ninety-second Congress, Hicks was assigned to the Committee on Education and Labor and the Committee on Veterans' Affairs. She was particularly interested in issues of education and proposed a system of tax credits for parents of children in private schools. She also sought a federal ban on busing to achieve desegregation. Although she called for the withdrawal of American troops in Southeast Asia, she supported President Nixon on a majority of votes before the House.

Soon after arriving in the House of Representatives, Hicks entered her second race for mayor of Boston, but this time she lost heavily to incumbent Kevin White. She also lost her bid for election to a second House term from a redrawn Ninth District in 1972. After returning to her law practice in Boston in 1973 she won election to another term on the Boston City Council. She is a resident of Boston.

MARJORIE SEWELL HOLT

(U.S. House of Representatives)

United States Representative
Republican of Maryland
Ninety-third–Ninety-ninth Congresses
January 3, 1973–January 3, 1987

After serving in local government and participating in state Republican Party business, Marjorie Holt spent much of her time in Congress focusing on issues of national defense and the armed services. As a member of the Committee on Armed Services during her entire service in the House and as a member of the Budget Committee in the Ninety-fifth

and Ninety-sixth Congresses, Holt was a persistent advocate of increased defense spending and improved benefits for armed services personnel. She supported development of the MX missile and the B-1 bomber while opposing programs for a nuclear freeze. In her final term in the House she had risen to be rank-

103

ing Republican on the Subcommittee on Procurement and Military Nuclear Systems.

Holt was born Marjorie Sewell in Birmingham, Alabama, on September 17, 1920. She attended Jacksonville (Florida) Junior College in 1940 and 1941 and received her LL.B. from the University of Florida College of Law in 1949. After practicing in Florida she moved to Maryland in the 1960s and continued to practice law in Anne Arundel County. She served two years as a supervisor of elections and from 1966 to 1972 served as clerk of the Anne Arundel County Circuit Court. At the same time she became involved in the Republican Party organization as a precinct leader and local campaign organizer. She served as counsel for the Maryland State Federation of Republican Women. Holt entered the Republican primary for the House seat from Maryland's Fourth District in 1972, and after defeating token opposition won the general election in the year of a Republican presidential landslide. She easily won reelection up until her decision to retire at the end of the Ninety-ninth Congress.

In Congress, Holt continued to emphasize her campaign theme of the need to reduce non-military spending. In 1978 she offered a Republican substitute budget proposal, and although the effort failed it became a standard party strategy in the future. Holt also was a strenuous opponent of busing schoolchildren as a means of achieving integration and in 1974 gained House approval for a constitutional amendment prohibiting the practice. Holt gained enough influence in the House Republican Party to win the chair of the Republican Study Committee by the beginning of her second term.

Following her resignation in 1987, Holt resumed the practice of law in Baltimore and is a resident of Severna Park, Maryland.

ELIZABETH HOLTZMAN

(U.S. House of Representatives)

United States Representative
Democrat of New York
Ninety-third–Ninety-sixth Congresses
January 3, 1973–January 3, 1981

After entering the campaign as a virtual unknown and relying largely on volunteers, Elizabeth Holtzman in 1972 toppled Emanuel Celler, a fifty year veteran of the House and powerful chairman of the Judiciary Committee. In her first term she gained a seat on the Judiciary Committee and won attention for her part in the hearings on the impeachment of President Nixon. Throughout her term in Congress, Holtzman earned a reputation as a thoughtful and effective legislator.

Holtzman is a native of Brooklyn, where she was born on August 11, 1941, and attended school. She graduated from Radcliffe College in 1962 and earned her J.D. from Harvard Law School in 1965. While a student she participated in civil rights work in Albany, Georgia. Holtzman returned to New York City where she practiced law and worked as an assistant to Mayor John Lindsay from 1967 to 1970. She also became involved in party politics as Democratic state committee member and district leader before her run for Congress.

Although the eighty-four year old Emanuel Celler maintained influence within the House of Representatives, by 1972 he had no district office in Brooklyn and was removed from local affairs. In a primary challenge that demonstrated her personal energy, Holtzman emphasized her commitment to constituent needs and her substantive differences with the incumbent who had blocked the Equal Rights Amendment in the Judiciary Committee and continued to support the war in Vietnam. She won the nomination by just over 600 votes and in the general election won a lop-sided victory over the Republican candidate and Celler, whose name remained on the Liberal Party ticket.

In addition to her work on the impeachment hearings in her initial term in the House, Holtzman in 1973 filed suit to halt American military action in Cambodia. A district court ruled the Cambodian invasion unconstitutional, but the Court of Appeals reversed the decision. As a member of the Judiciary Committee she also contributed to the formulation of new rules for the presentation of evidence in federal courts and worked to revise immigration laws. While continuing to serve on the Judiciary Committee, Holtzman also sat on the Budget Committee in the Ninety-fourth through Ninety-fifth Congresses. In 1978 she helped win an extension of the ratification deadline for the Equal Rights Amendment. She also helped secure a prohibition on sex discrimination in federal programs.

In 1980 Holtzman entered the Democratic primary for nomination to the Senate rather than seek reelection for a fifth term in the House. She won the heated contest for the nomination against Bess Myerson and her former boss, John Lindsay, but in the general election she lost to Republican Alfonse D'Amato. In 1981 she was elected district attorney of Brooklyn and served in that office until she was elected comptroller of New York City in November 1989.

NAN WOOD HONEYMAN

(Oregon Historical Society)

United States Representative
Democrat of Oregon
Seventy-fifth Congress
January 3, 1937–January 3, 1939

One of the New Deal's best congressional friends in the late 1930s was Nan Wood Honeyman of Oregon. She was born in West Point, New York, on July 15, 1881. After her father, adjutant of the United States Military Academy, resigned from the Army in 1883, he moved his family to Portland, Oregon, where his daughter, known as "Nanny," attended private schools and was graduated from St. Helen's Hall in 1898. She later attended the Finch School in New York City for three years, where she studied music and established her lifelong friendship with Franklin and Eleanor Roosevelt. In 1907 she married David T. Honeyman, a Portland hardware company executive.

In 1933 Honeyman served as president of the state constitutional convention which ratified the Twenty-first Amendment repealing Prohibition. From 1935 to 1937 she was a member of the Oregon House of Representatives and was a delegate to the Democratic national conventions of 1936 and 1940.

In 1936 Honeyman challenged incumbent Republican William A. Ekwall and independent candidate John A. Jeffrey in the race for representative from Oregon's Third District. The divided opposition and a Roosevelt landslide that held Republican challenger Alfred M. Landon to less than 30 percent of Oregon's popular vote contributed to her upset victory.

In the House Honeyman served on the Committee on Indian Affairs, the Committee on Irrigation and Reclamation, and the Committee on Rivers and Harbors, and was in all her legislative duties a dedicated supporter of the New Deal. Although her congressional career was thought to hold great promise due to her ties to the White House, her critics charged that she too often deferred to the national political concerns of President Roosevelt at the expense of constituent requests and such district business as legislation affecting the Bonneville Dam.

Honeyman ran for reelection in 1938 and despite campaign help from Interior Secretary Harold L. Ickes, who admired her stand on public power, she lost a close race to Homer D. Angell, who also defeated her in a rematch two years later.

In July 1941 the Multnomah County commissioners appointed Honeyman to fill a vacancy in the state senate, and she served until she resigned in October to become senior representative of the Pacific Coast Office of Price Administration. In May 1942 President Roosevelt appointed her collector of customs for the twenty-ninth district, Portland, a position she held until July 1953. She moved to Woodacre, California, in the mid-1960s and died there on December 10, 1970.

WINNIFRED SPRAGUE MASON HUCK

(U.S. House of Representatives)

United States Representative
Republican of Illinois
Sixty-seventh Congress
November 7, 1922–March 3, 1923

Winnifred Mason Huck was born in Chicago on September 14, 1882, and attended public schools there. When her father, William E. Mason was elected to the House of Representatives in 1890, she moved to Washington, D.C., where she graduated from Central High School. In 1904 she married civil engineer Robert W. Huck and lived with him in Salida, Colorado, and Chicago.

William E. Mason, who served in the Senate from 1897 to 1903 and returned to the House of Representatives from Illinois' at-large seat in 1917, died on June 16, 1921. Two weeks later, Huck announced that she would be a candidate in the April 1922 primary for nomination to the remainder of her father's term in the Sixty-seventh Congress as well as a full term in the Sixty-eighth. Although she was denied the endorsement of the Illinois Republican Women's Club, Huck narrowly won the primary for the vacant seat, but in her bid for nomination to a full term she lost to Henry R. Rathbone. In the special election of November 7, 1922, she defeated the Democratic nominee, Allen D. Albert. Huck was sworn in on November 20.

During her brief tenure in the Sixty-seventh Congress, Huck served on the Committee on Expenditures in the Department of Commerce, the Committee on Reform in the Civil Service, and the Committee on Woman Suffrage. She disdained the custom which required new members of Congress to remain silent and offered quotable remarks on a variety of issues. Huck, whose father had voted against entry into the war in Europe, defied popular opinion by calling for the release of sixty-two men imprisoned for seditious speeches and writings during the First World War.

In February 1923 Huck proposed legislation barring any United States trade with or financial concessions to nations that did not permit their citizens to participate in referendums on war declarations. She also introduced a concurrent resolution declaring the people of the Philippine Islands to be free and independent, championed self-government for Cuba and Ireland, and promoted a constitutional amendment requiring a direct popular vote for United States' involvement in any war requiring armed forces to be sent overseas.

Before the close of Huck's House career in March 1923, she entered the primary to fill the vacancy left by the death of Second District Representative James R. Mann in November 1922. Huck was defeated in the February 1923 primary by former state senator Morton D. Hull. Following the primary Huck charged that Hull had spent $100,000, exceeding the $5,000 limit on congressional campaign expenditures, and unsuccessfully called for a House investigation of his campaign.

Following her term in the House, Huck joined the political council of the National Women's Party and wrote a syndicated newspaper column. In 1925, her articles on the criminal justice system, prison conditions, and the rehabilitation of convicts created a sensation since they were based on her own undercover investigations. Ohio Governor Vic Donahey arranged for her to take an assumed name, stand convicted of theft, and spend four weeks in a women's prison before seeking out a series of odd jobs throughout the Northeast and Midwest. Huck continued her work in journalism and lecturing until her death in Chicago on August 24, 1936.

MURIEL BUCK HUMPHREY

(U.S. Senate Historical Office)

United States Senator
Democrat of Minnesota
Ninety-fifth Congress
January 25, 1978–November 7, 1978

For nine months, Muriel Humphrey carried out the work of her late husband, Hubert Humphrey, in the United States Senate. Minnesota Governor Rudy Perpich appointed Muriel Humphrey on January 25, 1978, to serve in her husband's Senate seat until a special election could be held to fill the remainder of his term. She took the oath of office on February 6. Although she declined to run for the special election, she used her brief tenure in Congress to speak out on a number of substantive issues. In her first speech as a senator, she urged ratification of the treaties turning over control of the Panama Canal to Panama and guaranteeing the canal's neutrality.

Humphrey served on the Committee on Foreign Relations and the Committee on Governmental Operations. On the Foreign Relations panel she voted in favor of President Carter's proposal to sell jet fighter planes to Egypt, Israel and Saudi Arabia. She was the sponsor of a successful amendment to the Civil Service Reform Act of 1978 which offered better job security to federal employees who exposed fraud or waste. She was a cosponsor of the joint resolution extending the deadline for ratification of the Equal Rights Amendment. In September of 1978, the Senate approved her amendment to the Department of Education Organization Act that changed the name of the Department of Health, Education and Welfare to the Department of Health and Human Services.

Muriel Fay Buck was born in Huron, South Dakota, on February 20, 1912, and attended Huron College. She resigned from the Senate on November 7, 1978, following the election of David Durenberger to serve the remainder of Hubert Humphrey's term. Since her retirement, she has remarried and lives in Excelsior, Minnesota, as Muriel Humphrey Brown.

VIRGINIA ELLIS JENCKES

(U.S. House of Representatives)

United States Representative
Democrat of Indiana
Seventy-third–Seventy-fifth Congresses
March 4, 1933–January 3, 1939

In her first campaign for public office, Virginia Jenckes defeated incumbents in both the Democratic primary and in the general election for the House seat from Indiana's Sixth District which had been redrawn to incorporate the incumbents' former districts. In her race for the first New Deal Congress, Jenckes promised to support the repeal of Prohibition in the hopes of encouraging an economic revival. As a founder and secretary of the Wabash and Maumee Valley Improvement Association and the manager of a farm, she was well aware of the impact of the Depression on the rural Indiana district.

Virginia Ellis was born on November 6, 1877, in Terre Haute, Indiana, where she attended school. Following her marriage in 1912 she helped manage her husband's farm, and with his death in 1921 she took responsibility for the 1,300 acre operation. When she entered the race for Congress in 1932 and traversed the district with her daughter as chauffeur, Jenckes emphasized local economic problems and the need for federal funding of flood control in the area.

Jenckes served on the Committee on Civil Service and the Committee on the District of Columbia throughout her three terms in the House. In the Seventy-third and Seventy-fourth Congresses, she also served on the Committee on Mines and Mining. Like many who served on the District of Columbia Committee, she found the work offered few rewards with her constituents. With the implementation of New Deal relief programs, Jenckes turned her attention to other matters. She strongly supported the work of the F.B.I. and warned of the dangers of communist indoctrination in the public schools of the nation's capital.

In 1938 Jenckes lost her seat to Republican Noble Johnson who had served in Congress from 1925 to 1931. Jenckes remained in Washington to work for the American Red Cross. She later gained brief attention for her role in aiding the escape of five priests from Hungary during the uprising of 1956. Jenckes died in Terre Haute on January 9, 1975.

NANCY L. JOHNSON

(Office of Representative Johnson)

United States Representative
Republican of Connecticut
Ninety-eighth–One Hundred First Congresses
January 3, 1983–present

Nancy Johnson used her experience in community and civic affairs as an effective foundation for her later career in elective politics. Before her election to the Connecticut Senate in 1976, she worked as a volunteer in local school programs, community children's services, and fund raising campaigns for libraries and charities. As a legislator she has continued to pursue a diverse agenda.

Johnson was born Nancy Lee on January 5, 1935, in Chicago, Ill. She attended the Lab School at the University of Chicago, received a B.A. from Radcliffe College in 1957, and subsequently attended the University of London. She moved to New Britain, Connecticut, in the 1960s. At the urging of the local Republican committee she successfully ran for state senate in 1976 and has remained in public office since.

Johnson won election to the open seat in Connecticut's Sixth District in 1982. During her first term in the House of Representatives she served on the Committee on Public Works and Transportation, the Veterans' Affairs Committee and the Select Committee on Children, Youth and Families. In the One Hundredth Congress she joined the Budget Committee and in the One Hundred First relinquished her other assignments for a spot on the influential Committee on Ways and Means.

Johnson's legislative concerns range from the protection of industries and jobs in her district to federal policy for child care and public health.

BARBARA CHARLINE JORDAN

(U.S. House of Representatives)

United States Representative
Democrat of Texas
Ninety-third–Ninety-fifth Congresses
January 3, 1973–January 3, 1979

In just three terms in the House of Representatives, Barbara Jordan earned national recognition as a defender of constitutional rights and champion of the needs of the underprivileged. Jordan represented the Eighteenth District of Texas which incorporated much of her hometown of Houston. She was born there February 21, 1936, and graduated from Phillis Wheatley High School. After graduating from Texas Southern University in Houston in 1956, she received a law degree from Boston University School of Law in 1959. Jordan entered law practice in Houston in 1960 and soon became involved in politics as an unsuccessful candidate for the state legislature in 1962 and 1964. Following work as administrative assistant to Harris County Judge Bill Elliott she finally won a seat in the Texas Senate in 1966. She became the first black to serve in the state senate since 1883 and continued to serve until 1972.

In 1972 Jordan and Andrew Young of Georgia became the first blacks elected to Congress from the South since 1898. In her first campaign for the House of Representatives, Jordan defeated Republican Paul Merritt for the seat from the newly-drawn Eighteenth District. She was appointed to the Committee on the Judiciary on which she served throughout her House service. In the Ninety-fourth and Ninety-fifth Congresses she also served on the Committee on Government Operations.

As a member of the Judiciary Committee in her freshman term, Jordan participated in the hearings on the resolution to impeach President Richard Nixon. She first gained national attention when she defended her vote for all five articles of impeachment as an act of constitutional responsibility. In 1976, Jordan became the first woman as well as the first black to serve as keynote speaker at a Democratic National Convention.

From her first days in Congress, Jordan called on her colleagues to extend the federal protection of civil rights. She offered civil rights amendments to legislation authorizing law enforcement assistance grants and joined seven other members of the Judiciary Committee in opposing Gerald Ford's nomination as vice president based on what they considered his weak civil rights record. When in 1975 Congress voted to extend the Voting Rights Act of 1965, Jordan sponsored legislation broadening the provisions of the act to include Hispanic Americans, native Americans, and Asian Americans. Among her other legislative accomplishments was the Consumer Goods Pricing Act of 1975.

Jordan declined to run for reelection to the House in 1978. Since retiring from politics in 1979 she has taught at the Lyndon B. Johnson School of Public Affairs at the University of Texas in Austin and has continued to speak on national affairs.

FLORENCE PRAG KAHN

United States Representative
Republican of California
Sixty-ninth–Seventy-fourth Congresses
March 4, 1925–January 3, 1937

Florence Prag Kahn was an early example of a widow who achieved a substantive congressional career of her own following election to her late husband's seat. In Kahn's six terms in the House she became an effective advocate of her district's interests and carried on much of her husband's legislative agenda.

The daughter of Polish immigrants, Florence Prag was born in Salt Lake City, Utah, on November 9, 1866, and moved shortly thereafter to San Francisco. Her father resumed business as a merchant and her mother began an extensive career in teaching, eventually serving on the city's board of education. Florence attended the University of

California at Berkeley and taught school before her marriage to Julius Kahn in 1899. Kahn, a German immigrant who worked as an actor before studying law, had served in the California legislature and first won election to the House of Representatives a few months before his marriage. With the exception of the Fifty-eighth Congress, he served in the House until his death in 1924 and served as chairman of the Committee on Military Affairs.

Florence Kahn worked closely with her husband, particularly in the final years of his service when illness prevented him from devoting full time to his duties. Julius Kahn was reelected to the Sixty-ninth Congress but died before the start of the Congress. Florence Kahn won the special election of February 17, 1925, to succeed him as California's Fourth District representative. She won reelection to the five succeeding Congresses and in the Seventy-first and Seventy-second Congresses succeeded her husband on the Military Affairs Committee. In her first term she served on the Committee on the Census, the Committee on Coinage, Weights, and Measures, the Committee on Education, and the Committee on Expenditures in the War Department. She also served on the War Claims Committee in the Seventieth Congress and the Appropriations Committee in the Seventy-third and Seventy-fourth Congress.

Pursuing her husband's commitment to military preparedness, Kahn managed to secure for California expanded military installations and other federal construction projects. She was instrumental in gaining congressional approval for the Bay Bridge connecting San Francisco and Oakland. Her support for the F.B.I. was so great that she became friends with J. Edgar Hoover who referred to her as the mother of the bureau. Much of Kahn's effectiveness in the House resulted from a vibrant and witty personality that made her presence known from the earliest days of her term. Her success in Congress, however, was not enough to withstand the Democratic landslide in the elections of 1938 when she lost her bid for a seventh term. Kahn retired to California where she lived until her death in San Francisco on November 16, 1948.

MARCY KAPTUR

(Office of Representative Kaptur)

United States Representative
Democrat of Ohio
Ninety-eighth–One Hundred First Congresses
January 3, 1983–present

Now in her fifth term in Congress, Marcy Kaptur has risen steadily in the committee system of the House of Representatives. Originally appointed to the Committee on Banking, Finance and Urban Affairs and the Veterans' Affairs Committee, in the One Hundred First Congress she took leave from the latter committee to take a seat on the Budget Commit-tee. Later in that Congress she resigned her previous assignments to accept a vacant seat on the Committee on Appropriations. In addition to her standing committee assignment, Kaptur serves on the Democratic Steering and Policy Committee that oversees committee assignments.

In her first bid for elective office, Kaptur was elected from Ohio's Ninth District in 1982 when she defeated incumbent Republican Edward Weber in a campaign that centered on the economic decline of the Toledo area district. Marcia Carolyn Kaptur was born in Toledo on June 17, 1946, and attended local schools. She received her B.A. from the University of Wisconsin in 1968, earned a masters in urban planning from the University of Michigan in 1974, and began doctoral studies at the Massachusetts Institute of Technology. She worked as an urban planner while pursuing much of her education. Kaptur served as an assistant for urban affairs for President Jimmy Carter from 1977 to 1979.

In the House of Representatives, Kaptur has concentrated on issues of home ownership, the protection of individuals' bank deposits and trading problems of special significance to industries in her district.

NANCY LANDON KASSEBAUM

United States Senator
Republican of Kansas
January 3, 1979–present

In 1978, Nancy Landon Kassebaum joined a crowded field in the Republican primary for nomination as U.S. senator from Kansas. As the daughter of Alfred Landon, the Republican presidential candidate of 1936, she was a member of one of the state's best-known Republican families, but she had little experience in public life, having served but two years on the school board of Maize, Kansas. Kassebaum, however, proved an effective and popular candidate and swept both the primary and the general election. She encountered no serious opposition in her reelection campaign in 1984.

Kassebaum was born Nancy Landon in Topeka, Kansas, on July 29, 1932. She graduated from the University of Kansas in 1954 with a B.A. and went on to earn her masters degree in history from the University of

Michigan in 1956. After raising a family she worked briefly as an assistant for Sen. James Pearson and helped manage a radio station in Wichita. From 1973 to 1975 she served on the local school board.

Since entering the Senate during the Ninety-sixth Congress in 1979, Kassebaum has served on the Committee on Banking, Housing, and Urban Affairs in the Ninety-sixth and One Hundred First Congresses, the Committee on the Budget in the Ninety-sixth through One Hundredth Congresses, the Committee on Foreign Relations from the Ninety-seventh through One Hundred First Congresses, the Committee on Commerce, Science and Transportation in the Ninety-sixth through One Hundredth Congresses, the Committee on Labor and Human Resources beginning in the One Hundred First Congress, the Select Committee on Aging in the Ninety-sixth through Ninety-eighth and One Hundred First Congresses, and the Select Committee on Ethics in the Ninety-ninth and One Hundredth Congresses.

While serving as chair of the Foreign Relations Subcommittee on African Affairs in the Ninety-seventh through Ninety-ninth Congresses, Kassebaum supported limited U.S. sanctions against South Africa. She also worked to restrict the type of assistance given the Contras in Nicaragua. Kassebaum has supported arms control negotiations and as a member of the Budget Committee in 1984 and 1987 worked to enact a bipartisan deficit reduction plan.

MAUDE ELIZABETH KEE

United States Representative
Democrat of West Virginia
Eighty-second–Eighty-eighth Congresses
July 17, 1951–January 3, 1965

The only woman representative from West Virginia, Maude Kee filled her husband's seat in Congress and after serving for fourteen years was succeeded by her son. She was born Maude Elizabeth Simpkins in Radford, Virginia, on June 7, 1895, and at an early age moved with her family to Roanoke, Virginia. She attended public and private schools in Montgomery County, Virginia, Roanoke, Washington, D.C., and Bluefield, West Virginia, before graduating from Roanoke Business College. She worked as a secretary for the business office of the *Roanoke Times* and as a court reporter for a law firm. She moved to Bluefield in 1925 and married attorney John Kee in September 1926.

Maude Kee was the author of "Washington Tidbits," a weekly column that was syndicated to West Virginia newspapers. After her husband was elected to the Seventy-third Congress as a Democratic Representative from West Virginia's Fifth District in 1932, Kee served as his executive secretary until he became chair of the Committee on Foreign Affairs in 1949. On July 17, 1951, Maude Kee won the special election held to fill the vacancy left by the death of John Kee on May 8. She was reelected six times by sizable majorities. Beginning with the Eighty-third Congress in 1953 her son James served as her administrative assistant.

Kee served on the Committee on Veterans' Affairs throughout the years of her House service and was a member of the Committee on Government Operations in the Eighty-fifth through Eighty-seventh Congresses and the Committee on Interior and Insular Affairs in the Eighty-eighth Congress. She chaired a Veterans' Affairs subcommittee on veterans hospitals and followed the liberal voting record of her husband. She was ardently pro-labor and supported many of the foreign and domestic policies of the Kennedy and Johnson administrations. Kee favored economic aid to Europe, the continuation of consumer price and federal rent controls and higher Social Security benefits with extended coverage. She opposed the use of the Taft-Hartley Act to end the steel strike in 1952 and voted against legislation granting ownership of submerged oil and gas deposits to the states. When she learned that the Woodrow Wilson Rehabilitation Center in Fishersville, Virginia, had room for a library but no books, she launched a campaign for books which resulted in the donation of over 10,000 texts.

Because of ill health Kee did not seek an eighth House term in 1964. She resided in Bluefield until her death on February 15, 1975.

EDNA FLANNERY KELLY

United States Representative
Democrat of New York
Eighty-first–Ninetieth Congresses
November 8, 1949–January 3, 1969

The longest-serving Congresswoman from New York, Edna Kelly, like many politicians of the New York Democratic organization, was a strong supporter of the federal government's social and economic programs and protective of United States interests in defense and foreign aid. She was born Edna Patricia Kathleen Flannery on August 20, 1906, in East Hampton, Long Island, New York, where she attended school. She received a B.A. degree from Hunter College in 1928. The same year she married attorney Edward L. Kelly, who served as a justice of the City Court and was active in Democratic politics in Brooklyn until he died in August 1942. Shortly after his death Eighteenth Assembly District leader Irwin Steingut placed Edna Kelly in charge of the women's auxiliary of the Madison Democratic Club.

Kelly moved on to a succession of party offices starting with her election in 1944 to the first of three terms on the Democratic executive committee of Kings County, New York. Steingut also secured her appointment as research director of the Democratic party in the state legislature in 1943 and she served there until her election to Congress. From 1956 to 1968 she was a member of the Democratic National Committee.

In July 1949 Kelly was chosen by Kings County Democratic leaders as their candidate to fill the vacancy caused by the death in April of Tenth District Representative Andrew L. Somers. She defeated opponents from the Republican and Liberal parties in November to win the House seat.

Kelly served on the Committee on Foreign Affairs and beginning with the Eighty-fourth Congress chaired its Subcommittee on Europe. She also chaired a special Subcommittee on the Canada-United States Inter-Parliamentary group and was secretary of the House Democratic Caucus. In 1967 Kelly was elected to the newly formed Committee on Standards of Official Conduct.

During the 1950s Kelly proposed legislation to extend rent control, provide working mothers with tax relief, and to require the Post Office to cancel mail with a stamp bearing the postmark, "In God We Trust." In April 1951 she introduced the first of her many bills to provide for equal pay for equal work for women. An implacable foe of communism, she sponsored a successful amendment to President Truman's 1952 request for $7.9 billion in foreign aid which suspended aid to Yugoslavia. The House also approved her amendment to the Agricultural Trade Development and Assistance Act of 1954 which outlawed the sale of farm surplus commodities to the Soviet Union or its satellites. She introduced resolutions calling for Irish unity and deploring religious persecution in Eastern Europe.

In 1955 Kelly introduced amendments to the Social Security Act to lower the retirement age for beneficiaries of old age and survivors' insurance benefits, and to the 1938 Fair Labor Standards Act to institute a $1.25 hourly wage. She sponsored resolutions to establish joint committees on intelligence and on consumers, and a select committee to investigate conditions in Veterans Administration hospitals. In 1963 she attached an amendment to ban economic aid to nations which did not permit the assistance to be verified or evaluated by the United States.

Kelly narrowly survived a primary challenge in 1966 from reformers opposed to New York City's entrenched Democratic organization. By 1968 the New York legislature had complied with court orders and divided Kelly's district between a new black-majority district, the Twelfth, and the Tenth District of Representative Emanuel Celler. Rather than retire she challenged Celler in the June primary, his first primary challenge since he entered Congress in 1923. Kelly mounted a spirited campaign but received only 32 percent of the vote in a three-way race.

She is a resident of Alexandria, Virginia.

BARBARA BAILEY KENNELLY

(Office of Representative Kennelly)

United States Representative
Ninety-seventh–One Hundred First Congresses
January 12, 1982–present

Barbara Kennelly gained a seat on the powerful Ways and Means Committee shortly after her special election to the House of Representatives in 1982. In the Ninety-ninth Congress Speaker Thomas P. "Tip" O'Neill, Jr. appointed her to the Democratic Steering and Policy Committee. These assignments gave her important legislative influence at an early stage in her congressional career.

Barbara Bailey was born in Hartford, Connecticut, on July 10, 1936, the daughter of John Bailey, long-time Democratic leader in the state and chairman of the Democratic National Committee in the 1960s. She received her B.A. from Trinity College in Washington, D.C., and a Masters in government from Trinity College in Hartford. Although she grew up surrounded by the world of politics, Kennelly did not hold public office until she was a member of the Hartford Court of Common Council from 1975 to 1979. She was elected secretary of state for Connecticut in 1979 and served in that office until she was elected to the Ninety-seventh Congress on January 12, 1982, to fill a vacancy caused by the death of First District Representative William R. Cotter.

In her first term in Congress, Kennelly served on the Committee on Government Operations and the Committee on Public Works and Transportation. In her second term she left those assignments to join the Committee on Ways and Means where she continues to serve as a member of the Subcommittees on Human Resources and Select Revenue Measures. In the One Hundredth Congress she became the first woman to serve on the Permanent Select Committee on Intelligence. From her position on Ways and Means she has pursued her legislative interest in child support, housing credits, welfare reform and tax reform.

MARTHA ELIZABETH KEYS

(U.S. House of Representatives)

United States Representative
Democrat of Kansas
Ninety-fourth–Ninety-fifth Congresses
January 3, 1975–January 3, 1979

In 1972 Martha Keys served as Kansas state coordinator of the George McGovern presidential campaign which was managed by her brother-in-law and future senator, Gary Hart. Although the Republican ticket had no trouble sweeping Kansas that year, Keys proved effective enough to make herself a viable candidate for a House seat in 1974

when Second District Republican William Roy resigned from the House to challenge Senator Robert Dole. In the general election she defeated state representative John C. Peterson to win election to Congress.

Keys was born Martha Elizabeth Ludwig in Hutchinson, Kansas, on August 10, 1930. After attending schools in Kansas City, Missouri, she enrolled at Olivet College in Kankakee, Illinois, and graduated with a B.A. from the University of Missouri at Kansas City in 1951.

As a freshmen member of the Ninety-fourth Congress, Keys won a prized seat on the Committee on Ways and Means. Much of her term, however, was spent maintaining support in her district where she faced a tough contest for reelection and narrowly defeated her Republican opponent. In 1978 she lost her seat to Jim Jeffries.

Keys served as a special adviser to the secretary of Health, Education and Welfare in 1979 and 1980 and as assistant secretary of Education in 1980 and 1981. She remained in Washington as a consultant and was director of the Center for a New Democracy in 1985 and 1986. She is a resident of Arlington, Virginia.

COYA GJESDAL KNUTSON

(U.S. House of Representatives)

United States Representative
Democrat of Minnesota
Eighty-fourth–Eighty-fifth Congresses
January 3, 1955–January 3, 1959

Coya Knutson's political career, largely devoted to the protection of the family farm, ended when her husband publicly called on her to resign from Congress and accused her of personal indiscretion. His celebrated "Coya, Come Home" letter, published in a local newspaper, overshadowed her substantive legislative record and eliminated much of her con-

stituent support. In her bid for a third term she lost the seat that she had won from a Republican incumbent in 1954.

The daughter of Norwegian immigrants who operated their own farm, Knutson was born Cornelia Gjesdal on August 22, 1912, in Edmore, North Dakota. She learned firsthand the problems facing a family farm before she

133

embarked on a career in education, public relations and social welfare. She graduated from Concordia College in Moorhead, Minnesota, and pursued graduate work in library science at the State Teachers' College in Moorhead and in music at the Juilliard School in New York. For sixteen years she taught in high schools in North Dakota and Minnesota. For two years during the Second World War, Knutson served as a field agent investigating issues of price support for the Agricultural Adjustment Administration. She also moved away from her teaching career when she worked for the Red Lake County welfare board from 1948 to 1950. Knutson's political career began in 1948 when she became chair of the Red Lake County Democratic-Farmer Labor party and served as a delegate at her first Democratic National Convention. In 1950 she won a seat in the Minnesota House of Representatives where she served until her election to Congress. As a member of the state assembly she was the author of legislation supporting dairy farmers and centered her attention on the issues of maternal care, education for the handicapped and mental health.

In 1954 when Knutson was the Democratic-Farmer Labor candidate to challenge Ninth District Representative Harold C. Hagen, she based her campaign on the need for better support of family farmers and a critique of the farm policy of Eisenhower and his secretary of agriculture, Ezra Taft Benson. After her election she became the first woman to win a seat on the Committee on Agriculture. In order to alleviate what she considered a crisis in the distribution of farm output, she advocated increased price supports for farm products, an extension of the food-stamp program for the distribution of farm surpluses, and a federally-supported school lunch program. She continued her attack on Benson and what she charged were his big-business farm policies.

As Knutson prepared to announce her campaign for reelection in 1958, her husband published a letter announcing that her career had devastated his home life and accusing her of involvement with a younger man who served as her administrative assistant. Her husband, widely reported to suffer from alcoholism, later claimed that political opponents of his wife had encouraged him to publicize his unhappiness with his wife's political career, but the incident irreparably damaged her campaign in which she became the only incumbent Democrat to lose a seat in 1958. After her loss she requested an investigation by the House Administration subcommittee on elections. That panel concluded that the letter had caused her defeat and the charges were false but found no evidence of political conspiracy.

Knutson, whose marriage predictably ended, failed in her attempt to win back her seat as the Democratic nominee in 1960. President Kennedy, grateful for her active campaign support, appointed her congressional liaison for the Office of Civilian Defense where she continued to serve until 1970. She made a final bid for return to the House of Representatives in nomination for a special election in 1977 but lost. Knutson is a resident of Bloomington, Minnesota.

KATHERINE GUDGER LANGLEY

(U.S. House of Representatives)

United States Representative
Republican of Kentucky
Seventieth–Seventy-first Congresses
March 4, 1927–March 3, 1931

Katherine Langley succeeded to her husband's seat in the House of Representatives following his conviction for conspiring to transport and sell liquor. John Wesley Langley won reelection in 1924 while his conviction was on appeal but was sentenced to the Federal Penitentiary in Atlanta before his term expired. In 1926 Katharine Langley ran for the House seat from Kentucky's Tenth District with the stated intention of vindicating her husband's name and carrying on his work.

By the time she won election to the Seventieth Congress, Langley was well-known in Washington and on Capitol Hill. Her father, James Madison Gudger, Jr., was a representative from North Carolina and while her husband served in the House, Katherine Langley worked as his secretary. From 1919 to 1925 she was clerk of the Committee on Public Buildings and Grounds, of which her husband was chairman. Katherine Langley was also an active member of the Kentucky Republican Party, serving as the first woman member of the state central committee and founder of the Women's Republican State Committee.

Although she represented a Republican district in an old unionist stronghold of eastern Kentucky, Katherine Langley was a native of North Carolina, raised in a Democratic family and active in the United Daughters of the Confederacy. She was born near Marshall, in Madison County, North Carolina, on February 14, 1888, and attended local schools. She graduated from the Woman's College in Richmond, Virginia, and after enrolling at Emerson College of Oratory in Boston, she taught expression at the Virginia Institute in Bristol. She married John Langley in 1903, and they moved to Pikeville, Kentucky, in 1905. Two years later her husband entered Congress.

When Katherine Langley entered the House of Representatives she was appointed to the Committee on Claims, the Committee on Immigration and Naturalization, and the Committee on Invalid Pensions. In the Seventy-first Congress she also served on the Committee on Education. Langley became the first woman to serve on the Republican Committee on Committees in 1930. At Katherine Langley's urging, President Coolidge granted her husband clemency on the informal promise that he never again stand for public office. John Langley not only betrayed his word to the president, he publicly declared his intention to seek his old House seat without informing his wife. She promptly announced that she had no intention of surrendering the seat to him. While her name remained on the ballot, the public row cost her enough votes to allow Democrat Andrew Jackson May to win the seat in 1930.

John Langley died in 1932 and Katherine served as railroad commissioner of the third Kentucky district from 1939 to 1942. She died in Pikeville, Kentucky, on August 15, 1948.

MARILYN LLOYD

United States Representative
Democrat of Tennessee
Ninety-fourth–One Hundred First Congresses
January 3, 1975–present

Marilyn Lloyd was elected to the House of Representatives in 1974. She defeated the Republican incumbent, Lamar Baker, in the general election. Lloyd has continued to win re-election as a Democrat in a district that normally votes Republican in presidential contests.

In her first term in the House, Lloyd won a spot on the Committee on Science, Space and Technology which has jurisdiction over much of the legislation related to the atomic energy facilities at Oak Ridge in her district. Since the Ninety-seventh Congress, she has chaired the Subcommittee on Energy Research and Development. Lloyd also served on the Committee on Public Works (later Public Works and Transportation) from the Ninety-fourth through the Ninety-ninth Congresses. Since the Ninety-eighth Congress she has sat on the Committee on Armed Services. She has served on the House Select Committee on Aging since her election to Congress in 1974 and was appointed chair of the Subcommittee on Housing and Consumer Interests in January 1990.

Lloyd was born Rachel Marilyn Laird in Fort Smith, Arkansas, on January 3, 1929. She attended schools in Texas and Kentucky and studied at Shorter College in Rome, Georgia. With her husband she was the co-owner and manager of a radio station in Dalton, Georgia. She also owned and operated an aviation company in Tennessee.

CATHERINE SMALL LONG

(U.S. House of Representatives)

United States Representative
Democrat of Louisiana
Ninety-ninth Congress
March 30, 1985–January 3, 1987

Catherine Long entered the Ninety-ninth Congress after winning the special election held March 30, 1985, to fill the vacancy left by the death of her husband, Gillis Long. After election to eight terms as representative from Louisiana's Eighth District, Gillis Long died on January 20, 1985. Cathy Long defeated four other candidates to win the seat for the remainder of the term. After being sworn in on April 4, she was appointed to the Committee on Public Works and Transportation and the Committee on Small Business.

Catherine Small was born in Dayton, Ohio, on February 7, 1924, and graduated from high school in Camp Hill, Pennsylvania. Long's early career ranged from the military to politics. After graduating from Louisiana State University in 1948, she worked as a pharmacist's mate in the U.S. Navy. She subsequently was a staff assistant to Senator Wayne Morse and Representative James G. Polk. Her political experience also included service as a delegate to Democratic National Conventions and membership on the Louisiana Democratic Finance Council and the state party's central committee.

As a representative, Long paid special attention to Louisiana's economic needs. She sought to preserve price supports for sugar and opposed an amendment to the Mississippi River and Tributaries Project bill that would have required local governments in the lower Mississippi Valley to share the costs of flood control, a program that the federal govern-ment long had recognized as of national concern. Long joined her colleagues in the Louisiana delegation in introducing legislation to authorize the Legal Services Corporation to make a grant to the Gillis W. Long Poverty Law Center at Loyola University in New Orleans.

Long was co-sponsor of the Economic Equity Act of 1985 which secured pension and health benefits for women and sought to restrict racial and sex discrimination in insurance practices. She also supported economic sanctions against South Africa and aid for Nicaraguan refugees.

Citing the burden of remaining campaign debts from her special election, Cathy Long declined to run for reelection in 1986.

JILL LYNNETTE LONG

(Office of Representative Long)

United States Representative
Democrat of Indiana
One Hundred First Congress
March 28, 1989–present

Jill Long's surprise victory in a special election for Indiana's Fourth District followed unsuccessful bids for the Senate in 1986 and for a House seat in the general election of 1988. Long was elected to the House on March 28, 1989, in a contest to fill the vacancy created when Dan Coats left the House after appointment to Dan Quayle's Senate seat. In a race in which party competition drew national attention, Long concentrated on local issues.

Long was born in Warsaw, Indiana, on July 15, 1952, and was raised on the family farm. She graduated from Valparaiso University in 1974 and received her M.B.A. in 1978 and Ph.D. in 1984 from Indiana University. Before election to Congress, Long worked as a profes-

141

sor of business at Indiana University and Valparaiso University. Her only prior political experience was as a member of the Valparaiso City Council from 1983 to 1986.

In 1986 Long challenged Dan Quayle in his successful campaign for a second Senate term. Two years later she faced off against Representative Dan Coats only to lose again to the Republican incumbent. In her third try for congressional office in as many election years, Long defeated Dan Heath, and she took the oath of office on April 5, 1989. In her first term she serves on Veterans' Affairs Committee, the Committee on Agriculture, and the Select Committee on Hunger.

ROSE McCONNELL LONG

(U.S. Senate Historical Office)

United States Senator
Democrat of Louisiana
Seventy-fourth Congress
January 31, 1936–January 3, 1937

The appointment and subsequent election of Rose Long to the Senate seat of her late husband followed a factional dispute that was convoluted even by the standards of Huey Long's Louisiana. After Huey Long's assassination in September 1935, the leaders of his political organization designated candidates for the primary of January 21, 1936, and the April elections. Governor O.K. Allen was nominated to fill out the remainder of Long's Senate term while the speaker of the Louisiana House of Representatives, Allen Ellender, would run for the succeeding six-year term. Richard W. Leche was chosen as candidate for governor, and Earl Long, Huey's brother, would displace the acting lieutenant governor,

143

James A. Noe. When Allen died before his election to the short Senate term, Noe succeeded him as governor and refused to carry out the plans of the Long organization that had snubbed him. He refused their requests to appoint Ellender, preferring to name Rose McConnell Long on January 31, 1936.

Rose Long was sworn in on February 10 and on April 21 she won the special election held to fill the remaining months in her husband's term. She took the oath of office a second time on May 19, 1936, and served until the end of the Seventy-fourth Congress. Her five committee assignments were Claims, Immigration, Interoceanic Canals, Post Offices and Post Roads, and Public Lands and Surveys. From her seat on Public Lands and Surveys she proposed a successful measure to enlarge the Chalmette National Park on the site of the battle of New Orleans. In March of 1936 she joined her Louisiana colleague, John H. Overton, and the senators from Arkansas and Texas to seek authorization of the attendance of the Marine Band at centennial celebrations in Arkansas and Texas and at the forty-sixth Confederate Reunion in Shreveport. Long's low-key service on committee and in the full Senate was in marked contrast to the flamboyance of her husband. She retired to Shreveport at the end of her term.

Rose McConnell was born in Greensburg, Indiana, on April 8, 1892, and moved with her family to Shreveport, Louisiana, in 1901. She married Huey Long in 1913 and worked as a secretary while he attended law school at Tulane University. Their son, Russell Long was elected to the Senate from Louisiana in 1948 and served until 1987. Rose Long died in Boulder, Colorado, on May 27, 1970.

NITA M. LOWEY

(Office of Representative Lowey)

United States Representative
Democrat of New York
One Hundred First Congress
January 3, 1989–present

Nita Lowey won election to her first term in Congress in 1988 when she defeated incumbent Joseph DioGuardi in New York's Twentieth District. The House race was the first bid for elective office by Lowey who served twelve years in the office of the secretary of state in New York.

A native of the Bronx, New York, Lowey was born Nita Melnikoff on July 5, 1937. After attending public schools in New York City, she graduated with a B.A. from Mount Holyoke College in 1959. Lowey returned to live in New York City and was involved in various local educational and political activities.

145

Lowey's entrance into public life followed her campaign work for Mario Cuomo in his bid for lieutenant governor in 1974. After losing the election and being appointed secretary of state, Cuomo named Lowey to the anti-poverty division of his office. She continued to work for the secretary of state until 1987, and eventually became assistant secretary of state, dealing with such issues as education, drug-abuse prevention, housing and child care.

While working in state government, Lowey moved to Westchester County and the Twentieth District where she defeated two rivals for the Democratic nomination for the House of Representatives in 1988. After entering the One Hundred First Congress in January of 1989, Lowey was appointed to the Committee on Education and Labor, the Committee on Merchant Marine and Fisheries, and the Select Committee on Narcotics Abuse and Control.

CLARE BOOTHE LUCE

(U.S. House of Representatives)

United States Representative
Republican of Connecticut
Seventy-eighth and Seventy-ninth Congresses
January 3, 1943–January 3, 1947

In an unparalleled career stretching across the worlds of journalism, the theater, politics, and diplomacy, Clare Boothe Luce found almost immediate success in every venture she undertook. One of the most notable, and noted, American women of the twentieth century, she displayed a genius for publicity that at times verged on self-promotion but always insured an audience for her opinions and secured an object for her ambitions. She and her husband, Time-Life publisher Henry Luce, were acquainted with the most powerful and influential leaders in this country and around the world and were themselves important influences on public opinion.

Clare Boothe was born April 10, 1903, in New York City, but far from the elite, sophisticated society she would captivate as an adult. Clare's father, an orchestra pit musician, left the family when she was eight. Her mother, a former chorus girl, struggled to provide Clare with the kind of opportunities normally reserved for far wealthier children. She took her daughter on a tour of Europe just before the outbreak of the First World War and sent her to St. Mary's School on Long Island and Miss Mason's School in Tarrytown where she graduated in 1919. Clare's formal education, however, was at best intermittent, and the precocious girl relied heavily on her mother's instruction and her own, insatiable reading habit.

Soon after her mother's marriage to Albert E. Austin, a wealthy doctor from Greenwich, Connecticut, Clare married the millionaire society figure, George Brokaw. The marriage ended in 1929 when Clare Boothe received a divorce on the grounds of mental cruelty and won custody of her only daughter. Despite a handsome settlement, Clare Boothe went to work for the publishing company of her friend Condé Nast. She was soon working as an editor of *Vanity Fair* and was made managing editor in 1933. A year later she resigned to devote full time to writing plays and enjoyed a string of Broadway successes, most notably *The Women* which was also made into a highly successful film.

In 1935 Clare Boothe married Henry Luce, the co-founder of *Time* magazine and a personality every bit as forceful as herself. Soon after they met, the couple collaborated on plans for a new publication, *Life* magazine. The marriage also led Clare Luce to take a more active interest in politics. Formerly a Democrat, she embraced her husband's support of the presidential campaign of Wendell Willkie in 1940. She also toured Europe as a *Life* correspondent in the early months of the Second World War and returned to publish her account of the outbreak of war, *Europe in the Spring*. (Dorothy Parker referred to this widely-read book as "All Clare on the Western Front".)

A legal resident of Greenwich, Connecticut, although more frequently an occupant of the Waldorf Towers in New York City, Clare Luce agreed to run for Congress in 1942 from Connecticut's Second District, a seat held by her late stepfather, Albert Austin, from 1939 to 1941. Luce easily won nomination by the Connecticut Republican Convention and in the general election narrowly ousted the Democratic incumbent. Although Luce ran as a critic of what she labeled Roosevelt's "soft" war policy, her clever comments and striking personality dominated the campaign.

Luce's arrival in Washington generated high expectations from a press and public familiar with her exceptional career. She failed in her effort to gain a seat on the Committee on Foreign Affairs, but was appointed to the Committee on Military Affairs. In a celebrated first speech before the House, she used the discussion of post-war air rights as an opportunity to malign Vice President Henry Wallace and his foreign policy ideas that she labeled "globaloney". Through the remainder of the war, her seat in Congress was a platform from which she attacked Roosevelt's foreign policy and management of the war effort. As a leading critic of the Democratic president, Luce was selected as keynote speaker at the Republican National Convention in 1944; the first woman so honored by either party. Her "G.I. Joe and G.I. Jim" speech was one of her frequent charges that Roosevelt had "lied us into war," and through mismanagement had caused undue American fatalities.

Luce won a close reelection contest against Democrat Margaret Connor in 1944. In the final months of the war she joined a congressional delegation touring Europe and was among those who inspected the recently-liberated concentration camp of Buchenwald. As hostilities ended, Luce increased her warnings about the threat from an aggressive Soviet Union and introduced a resolution urging Congress to acknowledge American responsibility for Soviet domination of Poland following the Yalta conference. During her two terms in Congress, Luce offered various resolutions such as those recommending racial equality in the armed services, independence for India, and the formation of a post-war military pact with Great Britain and France. She also introduced bills to end restrictions on immigration from China and to offer more affordable housing to veterans, but the details of the legislative process never engaged her full attention. She declined to run for reelection in 1946.

In the years following her resignation from Congress, Luce remained active in the Republican Party and as a writer and lecturer. After campaigning for Eisenhower in 1952, she declined the new president's offer to join the cabinet as secretary of labor and accepted his appointment of her as ambassador to Italy. Before her resignation in 1957 she participated in diplomatic negotiations concerning Italy's border with Yugoslavia and injected herself into Italy's domestic politics as a foe of the Communist Party. In 1959 Eisenhower nominated her as ambassador to Brazil, but she withdrew after a confirmation process marred by a bitter, personal confrontation with Oregon Senator Wayne Morse who recalled her wartime attacks on Roosevelt.

In 1964 Luce worked for the presidential candidacy of Barry Goldwater and briefly entered the race for the Conservative Party nomination for the Senate in New York. Luce was a member of the President's Foreign Intelligence Advisory Board under Nixon, Ford and Reagan. Following the death of her husband in 1967 she lived in Hawaii much of the year. With the return of a Republican administration in the 1980s, Luce moved to Washington where she lived until her death on October 9, 1987.

GEORGIA LEE LUSK

United States Representative
Democrat of New Mexico
Eightieth Congress
January 3, 1947–January 3, 1949

For a generation, Georgia Lusk helped to shape the politics and educational policies of her native state. She was born Georgia Lee Witt on a ranch near Carlsbad, New Mexico, on May 12, 1893. After graduation from Carlsbad High School in 1912 she attended Highlands University in Las Vegas, New Mexico, and Colorado State Teachers College at Gree-

ley. She graduated from the New Mexico State Teachers College in Silver City in 1914. The following year she married rancher-banker Dolph Lusk and taught school in Eddy County.

When her husband died in 1919 Georgia Lusk became manager of the family ranch while continuing to teach and raise her children. In 1924 she was elected superintendent of Lea County and served in that capacity until 1929. After losing an initial bid for state superintendent of public instruction in 1928, she won the first of two successive terms in 1930 and served from 1931 to 1935. During 1941 and 1942 Lusk was a rural school supervisor in Guadalupe County. She again served as state superintendent from 1943 to 1947. While serving in that post Lusk provided New Mexico public schools with free textbooks and successfully lobbied the state legislature to fund a school construction plan, raise teacher salaries and institute a teachers' retirement program.

Lusk attended the Democratic national conventions of 1928 and 1948 as a New Mexico delegate and took part in the 1944 White House Conference on Rural Education. In 1946 she entered the campaign for the Democratic nomination for one of New Mexico's two at-large seats in the House of Representatives. She won the primary over six rivals and was the leading vote-getter in the general election.

As a member of the Committee on Veterans' Affairs, Lusk supported many of the Truman administration's domestic programs (although she voted to override President Truman's veto of the Taft-Hartley Act) and was a staunch backer of the administration's foreign policy proposals, voting for assistance to Greece and Turkey and endorsing universal military training. She also supported establishment of a cabinet-level department of education.

Lusk ran for renomination to her at-large seat in the June 1948 primary but fell short of the vote received by former Governor John E. Miles and incumbent Representative Antonio M. Fernandez. In September 1949 President Truman appointed her to the War Claims Commission, where she served with other Democratic appointees until their dismissal by President Eisenhower in December 1953.

Returning to New Mexico, Lusk was elected to two additional terms as state superintendent and served from 1955 to 1960. She died in Albuquerque on January 5, 1971.

KATHRYN O'LAUGHLIN McCARTHY

United States Representative
Democrat of Kansas
Seventy-third Congress
March 4, 1933–January 3, 1935

Kathryn O'Laughlin defeated an incumbent Republican to win election to the House of Representatives in 1932 only to lose her bid for reelection two years later. She focused her campaign on the devastated agricultural economy of western Kansas and proposed various federal policies to relieve the plight of farmers and ranchers. Before the Seventy-third

Congress opened in March of 1933, she married Kansas state senator Daniel McCarthy and used his name after taking office.

Kathryn Ellen O'Laughlin was born near Hays, Kansas, on April 24, 1894, and attended rural schools and the State Teachers College in Hays. She left the state to attend law school at the University of Chicago and after

153

graduation she practiced law in Chicago. She returned to Hays to continue practice in 1928. At the same time she participated in the Democratic Party organization in Kansas and in 1931 entered the Kansas House of Representatives. In 1932 she defeated Republican incumbent Charles Sparks for the House seat from Kansas' Sixth District.

After taking her seat in the Seventy-third Congress, McCarthy protested her assignment to the Committee on Insular Affairs and requested a seat on the Committee on Agriculture which she considered more relevant to the needs of her constituents. The Committee on Ways and Means, responsible for Demo-cratic assignments, refused her demand but transferred her to the Committee on Education where she sought increased federal funding for vocational schools. McCarthy generally endorsed the New Deal legislative program and was particularly supportive of the Agriculture Adjustment Act which she hoped would bring relief to the farmers of Kansas. In the election of 1934, she faced the farmers' dissatisfaction with the bureaucratic requirements of the AAA and lost her bid for another term. McCarthy returned to her law practice in Kansas and later owned a car dealership. She continued to attend Democratic Conventions. She died in Hays, Kansas, on January 16, 1952.

RUTH HANNA McCORMICK

United States Representative
Republican of Illinois
Seventy-first Congress
March 4, 1929–March 3, 1931

As a young girl, Ruth Hanna McCormick learned of politics through her father, Marcus Alonzo Hanna, the wealthy industrialist and powerful leader in the Republican party of the late-nineteenth century. As an adult, McCormick moved out of her father's shadow to establish herself as a stalwart campaigner and influential participant in Republican politics. She was born in Cleveland on March 27, 1880. After attending private schools in Cleveland, the Masters School in Dobbs Ferry, New York, and Miss Porter's School in Farmington, Connecticut, she ignored her family's wish that she attend college and worked instead as a personal secretary for her father when he became a United States senator from Ohio in 1899.

In June 1903 Ruth Hanna married Medill McCormick who would serve as a Republican state legislator, congressman, and senator from Illinois from 1912 until his death in 1925. Both husband and wife soon became interested in the Progressive movement and efforts to alleviate living conditions among the poor in the inner cities. They briefly resided at the University of Chicago Settlement, an experience that deepened Ruth McCormick's concern for the welfare of women and children. Unable to purchase a special type of milk needed by one of her children and appalled by the unhygienic condition of many Illinois dairies, she opened a dairy and breeding farm near Byron, Illinois, to produce sanitary milk for invalids and children.

In 1912 she and her husband departed from their families' traditional Republicanism to support the Progressive Party's campaign for former president Theodore Roosevelt. In the years before United States involvement in the First World War, she was an advocate of American preparedness through unofficial military training and, like her husband, was later an impassioned opponent of the League of Nations.

During the 1920s McCormick found increasing influence within the Republican Party. She chaired the first woman's executive committee of the Republican National Committee and was an associate member of the National Committee from 1919 until 1924, when she became the first elected national committeewoman from Illinois. She enhanced her visibility and political prospects by sponsoring a state-wide network of women's Republican clubs that could easily be converted into a campaign organization if the need arose.

In 1928 McCormick left her National Committee post to aid the presidential campaign of Illinois Governor Frank O. Lowden and to run for one of Illinois' two at-large seats in the House of Representatives. A tireless campaigner and excellent public speaker, she led the Republican state ticket, finishing ahead of nine other candidates. After being sworn in to office, she was appointed to the Committee on Naval Affairs.

McCormick had barely settled into her House seat in the Seventy-first Congress when she announced that rather than run for reelection in 1930 she would be a candidate for the Republican nomination to the United States Senate. She won the April primary over incumbent Charles S. Deneen who had beaten her husband for renomination in 1924 and in the general election faced former Senator James Hamilton Lewis who had lost his Senate seat to her husband in 1918. McCormick's prospects for victory were dimmed by the unpopularity of President Hoover's response to the Depression, her continued support of Prohibition, and accusations by members of Senator Gerald P. Nye's Select Committee to Investigate Contributions and Expenses of Senatorial Candidates that she was trying to buy her way into the Senate through lavish campaign expenditures. Running in a year that saw Republicans lose fifty-three House and eight Senate seats, McCormick managed to secure only 33 percent of the vote.

Although her career as an elective officeholder came to an end, McCormick had no intention of retiring from public affairs. In March 1932 she married Albert Gallatin Simms, a former Republican congressman from New Mexico who also served in the Seventy-first Congress, and devoted much of her time to operating her dairy, two newspapers and a radio station, a Colorado cattle and sheep ranch, and her school for girls in Albuquerque, New Mexico. In 1940 McCormick joined J. Russell Sprague, the Long Island Republican leader, to manage Thomas E. Dewey's presidential campaign. At the national convention at Philadelphia she and Sprague unsuccessfully attempted to persuade Robert Taft to accept the vice-presidential nomination on a ticket with Dewey in the hopes of stopping the nomination of Wendell Willkie. After Willkie won the nomination, McCormick initially supported his campaign but later denounced him for his support of military aid to Great Britain. During the Second World War, McCormick continued to advise Dewey and assisted his unsuccessful presidential campaign of 1944. She died in Chicago on December 31, 1944.

CLARA GOODING McMILLAN

(U.S. House of Representatives)

United States Representative
Democrat of South Carolina
Seventy-sixth Congress
November 7, 1939–January 3, 1941

Clara McMillan was the choice of Democratic Party leaders in South Carolina to succeed her late husband, Thomas S. McMillan, in the House seat from the First District. Against two weak opponents, she won the special election of November 7, 1939, and took her seat in Congress at the opening of the third session of the Seventy-sixth Congress on January 3, 1940. In a session that lasted a full year, McMillan served on the Committee on Patents, the Committee on Public Buildings and Grounds and the Committee on the Election of President, Vice President, and Representatives in Congress.

The threat of American involvement in the war in Europe dominated the business of the final session of the Seventy-sixth Congress. McMillan made clear her support of military preparedness and spoke in favor of the Burke-Wadsworth Selective Service Bill which established the nation's first peacetime draft. She also introduced legislation to provide for the designation of individual domiciles in income tax returns and to allow local police officers to mail firearms for repairs.

McMillan declined renomination for a full term in the face of the candidacy of L. Mendel Rivers, who went on to represent the district for nearly thirty years. McMillan continued in governmental service with the National Youth Administration, the Office of War Information, and from 1946 to 1957 as information liaison officer with the Department of State.

Clara Gooding was born in Brunson, South Carolina, on August 17, 1894. After schooling in her hometown, she attended the Confederate Home College in Charleston and Flora MacDonald College in Red Springs, North Carolina. McMillan retired to Barnwell, South Carolina, where she died on November 8, 1976.

HELEN DOUGLAS MANKIN

(U.S. House of Representatives)

United States Representative
Democrat of Georgia
Seventy-ninth Congress
February 12, 1946–January 3, 1947

In her short term of service in the House of Representatives, Helen Douglas Mankin carried on her long-running efforts to reform Georgia politics and offer black citizens a greater voice in public affairs. She was born on September 11, 1894, in Atlanta, Georgia, where she attended school. After graduation from Washington Seminary in 1913, she at-tended Rockford (Illinois) College, where she received her A.B. in 1917. She interrupted law studies with her father to volunteer for nursing service in the First World War, first with the Medical Women's National Association in Washington and for the year following the armistice as an ambulance driver for the American Women's Hospital No. 1 in France. On

159

her return to the United States, she and her sister embarked on a widely publicized cross-country trip by automobile.

Helen Douglas graduated from Atlanta Law School, an institution organized by her father, in 1920 and commenced practice in Atlanta. She frequently aided poor or black clients while supplementing her income through lectures at Atlanta Law School. She was women's manager of I.N. Ragsdale's campaign for mayor of Atlanta in 1927. In September 1927 she married Guy M. Mankin and traveled with him as he worked as an electric power system designer in Cuba, Brazil and Argentina until their return to Atlanta in 1933.

In 1935 Mankin, who chaired the Georgia Child Labor Committee, unsuccessfully urged the state legislature to ratify the proposed child labor amendment to the Constitution. The following year she won herself a seat in the state assembly and served until her election to Congress. She proposed an investigation of Governor Eugene Talmadge's administration of the State highway department and voted for constitutional, educational, electoral, labor, and prison reforms.

When Fifth District Representative Robert Ramspeck announced his retirement from the House, Mankin entered the race to succeed him. In the special election of February 12, 1946, she narrowly won the seat, largely on the basis of support from black voters who were normally barred from party primaries but eligible to vote in the special election. For the remainder of the Seventy-ninth Congress she served on the Committees on Civil Service, Claims, Elections, and Revision of the Laws. In contrast with many of her Georgia colleagues, she opposed funding for the House Committee on Un-American Activities and favored an end to the poll tax. In the Democratic primary of July 1946 Mankin outpolled her opponent, James C. Davis, by more than 11,000 votes, but the state's county unit system, which heavily favored rural districts, awarded her six unit votes for carrying Fulton County, while Davis received eight for carrying two less populous counties. Despite attempts by the Georgia Democratic Executive Committee to place her name on the ballot as the Democratic nominee, Talmadge, the Democratic nominee for a fourth term as governor, used his influence to remove Mankin's name. She remained in the race as a write-in candidate and in spite of intimidations by white supremacy groups and various voting frauds received 38 percent of the vote. When Mankin challenged Davis' victory before the House Administration Committee's Subcommittee on Privileges and Elections, the Subcommittee voted to reject her charges.

Following her departure from Congress Mankin returned to her law practice and continued her fight against the county unit system. In March 1950 the United States District Court in Atlanta ruled against her, a decision upheld in May by the United States Supreme Court which would not rule the county unit system unconstitutional until 1962. Mankin served as a volunteer in the presidential campaign of Adlai Stevenson in 1952 and as a fund raiser for Israel. On July 25, 1956, she died in College Park, Georgia, following an automobile accident.

LYNN MARTIN

United States Representative
Republican of Illinois
Ninety-seventh–One Hundred First Congresses
January 3, 1981–present

After nearly a decade in the House of Representatives, Lynn Martin has established herself as a Republican Party leader on and off Capitol Hill. In 1984 and 1986 she won election as vice chair of the Republican Conference in the House, the first time a woman held a position in the congressional party's hierarchy. In 1984 she also helped then Vice

President George Bush prepare for his debate with Martin's House colleague, Geraldine Ferraro. In the House chamber, Martin has regularly been a floor manager for the Republican party.

Martin began her first term in Congress with an appointment to the influential Budget Committee where she served for three

Congresses. In the Budget Committee negotiations of 1986, Martin led her party delegation and was largely responsible for acceptance of a Republican-sponsored reconciliation bill that year. Martin also served on the Committee on House Administration in the Ninety-seventh and Ninety-eighth Congresses, the Committee on Public Works and Transportation in the Ninety-eighth Congress, and the Committee on Armed Services in the Ninety-ninth and One Hundredth Congresses. In the One Hundred First Congress she gained a widely-sought seat on the Committee on Rules.

Martin's congressional career followed a decade of officeholding on the local and state level. Born Lynn Morley in Evanston, Illinois, on December 26, 1939, she attended schools in Chicago and received a B.A. from the University of Illinois in 1960. After working as a high school teacher, Martin was elected in 1972 to the Winnebago County (Illinois) Board and four years later won a seat in the Illinois House of Representatives. She moved on to the state senate in 1979. When Representative John Anderson's decision to run for president in 1980 opened the House seat in Illinois' Sixteenth District, Martin declared her candidacy and won against four Republicans in the primary and then won the general election.

In 1989 Martin announced her intention to run for senator from Illinois in 1990 rather than seek reelection to the House of Representatives.

CATHERINE DEAN MAY

(U.S. House of Representatives)

United States Representative
Republican of Washington
Eighty-sixth–Ninety-first Congresses
January 3, 1959–January 3, 1971

The first woman House Member from Washington, Catherine May represented a largely agricultural region and devoted many of her twelve years in Congress to the protection and improvement of farm income. She was born Catherine Dean Barnes on May 18, 1914, in Yakima, Washington. She graduated from Yakima Valley Junior College in 1934

before receiving a B.A. in 1936 and a five-year degree in education in 1937 from the University of Washington. She also studied speech at the University of Southern California in 1939 and was an English teacher at Chehalis, Washington, from 1937 to 1940.

In the early 1940s Barnes worked as a women's editor and news broadcaster in

Tacoma, Washington, as a writer and broadcaster of special events in Seattle, and as director of a radio department for a Seattle advertising agency and a Seattle insurance company. In January 1943 Barnes married John O. May and the next year became a writer and assistant commentator for the National Broadcasting Company in New York City. She returned to Yakima in 1946 and was women's editor for a radio station from 1948 to 1957. She was also an office manager and medical secretary for the Yakima Medical Center.

May was elected to the Washington legislature in 1952 and served until 1958. When eight-term Representative Otis H. Holmes decided not to stand for reelection from Washington's Fourth District in 1958, May entered the race and defeated Democrat Frank LeRoux. She served on the Committee on Agriculture throughout her House career and on the Committee on the District of Columbia and the Committee on Atomic Energy in the Ninety-first Congress.

Although May usually supported the Eisenhower administration during her first term, in September 1959 she joined the majority in the first override of an Eisenhower veto when the House voted to enact a $1.1 billion public works appropriation bill. Two years later she broke with most of her fellow Republicans and supported federal funding of power trans-mission lines for the Upper Colorado Basin Project's electric plants. Along with other Republican representatives from her state, she sought in vain to preserve congressional authorization for a plutonium reactor at Hanford, Washington.

Throughout her congressional career May attempted to encourage domestic production of beet sugar, an important industry in her district. She favored establishment of a special fee on imported sugar and in 1964 proposed a higher permanent quota for domestic sugar beets. She co-sponsored joint resolutions in 1967 to establish a United States World Food Study and Coordinating Commission and a Select Committee on Standards and Conduct. During 1970 May was sponsor of the Nixon administration's proposal to provide free food stamps to families with monthly incomes of less than thirty dollars.

May ran for a seventh term in 1970 but was defeated by Mike McCormack. She was remarried to Donald Bedell in November 1970 and appointed by President Nixon to the United States International Trade Commission, where she served from 1971 to 1981. In 1982 she was appointed a Special Consultant to the President on the 50 States Project. She is currently president of Bedell Associates and is a resident of Palm Desert, California.

JAN MEYERS

(Office of Representative Meyers)

United States Representative
Republican from Kansas
Ninety-ninth–One Hundred First Congresses
January 3, 1985–present

Jan Meyers learned of the needs of her Kansas district through more than fifteen years' experience in city government and the state legislature. From 1967 to 1972 she was a member of the Overland Park City Council, serving as president for two years. For the next twelve years she was a state senator, rising to be chair of the Public Health and Welfare Committee and the Local Government Committee. Meyers also worked in various statewide Republican campaigns.

Meyers was born in Lincoln, Nebraska, on July 20, 1928, and was raised in Superior, Nebraska. She graduated with an Associate Fine Arts degree from William Woods College in Fulton, Missouri, in 1948 and with a B.A.

from the University of Nebraska in 1951. Following college she worked in advertising and public relations.

Before her campaign for the House of Representatives, Meyers entered the Republican primary for U.S. Senate in 1978 but lost to Nancy Kassebaum. When Representative Larry Winn, Jr. retired in 1984, Meyers won the party nomination and the Third District seat in Congress. In her first term she was appointed to the Committee on Science and Technology, the Committee on Small Business, and the Select Committee on Aging. In the One Hundredth Congress, Meyers transferred from Science and Technology to the Committee on Foreign Affairs. As a member of this committee she has concentrated on efforts to halt the international drug trade. In the One Hundred First Congress she serves as vice chair of the Energy and Environment Study Conference.

HELEN STEVENSON MEYNER

(U.S. House of Representatives)

United States Representative
Democrat of New Jersey
Ninety-fourth–Ninety-fifth Congresses
January 3, 1975–January 3, 1979

A distant cousin of United Nations ambassador and two-time presidential nominee Adlai E. Stevenson, Helen Day Stevenson was born in New York City on March 5, 1929. She graduated from Rosemary Hall High School in Greenwich, Connecticut in 1946. From 1946 to 1950 she attended Colorado Springs College. She served in Korea as an American Red Cross field worker from 1950 to 1952, was a guide at the United Nations from 1952 to 1953, and a consumer advisor for an airline from 1953 to 1956.

In 1957 Stevenson married Robert B. Meyner, who had been elected in 1953 as New Jersey's first Democratic governor in a decade. After her husband left office in 1962,

Meyner began to write a twice-weekly column for the *Newark Star-Ledger* which continued until 1969. She also conducted a New Jersey and New York City television interview program from 1965 to 1968. Beginning in 1971 she was a member of the New Jersey State Rehabilitation Commission.

Meyner's political career began improbably in July 1972 when the Democratic nominee for New Jersey's Thirteenth District seat withdrew because he failed to meet a seven-year citizenship criteria for public office. Meyner, who had been writing a biography of author Katherine Mansfield, entered the contest upon the request of the Democratic state committee but lost to Republican Joseph J. Maraziti. In 1974 she defeated Maraziti for election to the Ninety-fourth Congress.

During her two terms in the House, Meyner served on the Committee on the District of Columbia, the Committee on Foreign Affairs and the Select Committee on Aging. She opposed efforts by some non-aligned nations to suspend or expel Israel from the United Nations. She also condemned the 1975 U.N. resolution equating zionism with racism but differed with those who urged the United States

to withdraw from the organization. Meyner voted to form a State Department board to explore the establishment of a center for conflict resolution and introduced an amendment to a Philippines assistance bill reducing aid by $5 million in an attempt to curtail human rights abuses by that nation's government.

Meyner was also concerned with the economic needs of her state. Along with other members of New Jersey's congressional delegation, she saved the Picatinny Arsenal in her district from closure and the facility was soon designated as the headquarters of a new armament development center. She tried to sustain New Jersey's textile industry in the face of competition from foreign imports and participated in 1978 Select Committee on Aging hearings on poor conditions in boarding homes for senior citizens. In late 1976 she lobbied Democratic members of the state senate, urging them not to rescind New Jersey's endorsement of the Equal Rights Amendment to the Constitution.

Meyner was defeated for reelection in 1978 by James A. Courter. She continues to serve on the State Rehabilitation Commission and is a resident of Princeton, New Jersey.

BARBARA ANN MIKULSKI

(Office of Senator Mikulski)

Democrat of Maryland
United States Representative
Ninety-fifth–Ninety-ninth Congress
January 3, 1977–January 3, 1987
United States Senator
January 3, 1987–present

Since she first became involved in a citizen's lobbying effort in the 1960s, Barbara Mikulski has advanced steadily through the world of Baltimore politics and Capitol Hill. She emerged as a leader of the popular movement to halt construction of a proposed highway through several established Baltimore neighborhoods. Following the success of the anti-highway movement, Mikulski was elected to a seat on Baltimore's City Council in 1971 and served with that body for five years.

In her first attempt at congressional office, she accepted the Democratic nomination to challenge Senator Charles Mathias in 1974. Mikulski failed to unseat the popular incumbent, but she was well-positioned in 1976 to seek the Third District House seat of Paul Sarbanes who declined renomination in order to mount his successful Senate campaign. Mikulski won a crowded primary and went on to her first of five easy victories in the heavily-Democratic district.

Mikulski arrived in the House with a thorough understanding of her native Baltimore where she was born July 20, 1936. She attended local parochial schools and graduated with a B.A. from Mount St. Agnes College in 1958. In 1965 she received a masters of social work from the University of Maryland School of Social Work. Before entering politics, she worked with Catholic charities and the Baltimore Welfare Department.

During her House career, Mikulski served as a member of the Committee on Merchant Marine and Fisheries in the Ninety-fifth through Ninety-ninth Congresses, the Committee on Interstate and Foreign Commerce in the Ninety-fifth and Ninety-sixth Congresses and its successor, the Committee on Energy and Commerce, in the two following Congresses. Mikulski pursued in the House the same sort of issues that attracted her to public affairs in Baltimore. She proposed or supported legislation dealing with child care, women's rights, national health insurance and consumer protection.

When Charles Mathias announced his retirement from the Senate, Mikulski decided to risk her safe seat in the House and vie for the Senate seat that eluded her in 1974. In the Democratic primary of 1986 she faced her House colleague Michael Barnes and Maryland's governor Harry Hughes. Working from a well-established political base in Baltimore, Mikulski won 50 percent of the primary vote and easily defeated Republican Linda Chavez in the general election.

As a senator, Mikulski sits on the Appropriations Committee, the Labor and Human Resources Committee, and the Small Business Committee. These assignments and her chairmanship of the Appropriations Subcommittee on VA, HUD and Independent Agencies allow her to continue her legislative work on social issues.

PATSY TAKEMOTO MINK

(U.S. House of Representatives)

United States Representative
Democrat of Hawaii
Eighty-ninth–Ninety-fourth, One Hundred First Congresses
January 3, 1965–January 3, 1977,
September 22, 1990–present

In her long and varied political career, Patsy Mink has been an effective champion of civil rights for women and minorities and of governmental support of educational opportunities. Born Patsy Matsu Takemoto on December 6, 1927, in the village of Paia on Maui, she graduated from a local high school and attended Wilson College in Chambersburg, Pennsylvania, and the University of Nebraska before returning to the University of Hawaii at Honolulu where she graduated in 1948. She earned her law degree at the University of Chicago in 1951 and opened her own practice in Hawaii. She also lectured at the law school of the University of Hawaii and served as attorney of the Hawaii House of Representatives in 1955.

Mink became involved in politics with the Young Democrats and served as a delegate to the Democratic National Convention in 1960 when as a member of the platform committee she helped negotiate adoption of the civil rights plank. She already had won election to the Hawaii House of Representatives in 1956 and to the state senate in 1958. In the state legislature she concentrated on education issues and equal pay for equal work while she continued her work in the statehood movement.

In Hawaii's first congressional elections after statehood, Mink failed to gain the Democratic nomination for the at-large seat in the House of Representatives. In 1964 she won the nomination and the general election for one of Hawaii's two House seats. As a member of Congress she successfully sought a seat on the Committee on Education and Labor where she served through the Ninety-fourth Congress. In her second term she also joined the Committee on Interior and Insular Affairs and in the Ninety-third and Ninety-fourth Congresses served on the Budget Committee.

Mink's fortunate committee assignments allowed her to concentrate on the same issues that had been the focus of her attention in the state legislature. Among the various education acts she introduced or sponsored were the first child care bill and legislation establishing bilingual education, student loans, special education, head start and numerous other programs. As a member of Interior and Insular Affairs she supported the economic and political development of the Trust Territory in the Pacific. As chair of the Subcommittee on Mines and Mining she was the primary author of the Surface Mining and Reclamation (Strip-mining) Act and the Mineral Leasing Act of 1976. During the Johnson presidency, Mink was a strong supporter of the administration's domestic program, but she was an early critic of the American military buildup in Vietnam. She refused to support the president's request for a tax increase in 1967 for fear that the new revenues would be used for military action rather than the expansion of social programs. Mink continued to defend the equal rights of women and was one of the earliest critics of President Nixon's nomination to the Supreme Court of G. Harrold Carswell who had denied women's employment rights as an appellate judge.

In 1976 Mink decided to seek the Democratic nomination for the U.S. Senate rather than run for reelection to a seventh term in the House. After losing that contest to Spark Matsunaga, Mink remained actively involved in government and politics. She served as assistant secretary of state for oceans and international environmental and scientific affairs in 1977 and 1978. For the next three years she was president of the Americans for Democratic Action. Mink returned to Hawaii and was elected to the Honolulu City Council on which she served from 1983 to 1987 and was chair from 1983 to 1985.

Mink returned to the House of Representatives in 1990 when she won a special election held September 22, to fill the vacancy in the Second District left by the resignation of Daniel Akaka following his appointment to the Senate. She once again serves on the Committee on Education and Labor and is also a member of the Committee on Government Operations. On the same day as the special election Mink won the Democratic nomination for the Second District seat in the One Hundred Second Congress.

SUSAN MOLINARI

(Office of Representative Molinari)

United States Representative
Republican of New York
One Hundred First Congress
March 20, 1990–present

Susan Molinari entered Congress as a result of a special election of March 20, 1990, held to fill the vacancy in New York's Fourteenth District left when her father, Guy Molinari, resigned to become Staten Island Borough president. She took the oath of office as a member of the One Hundred First Congress on March 27, 1990, and received assignments to the Committee on Public Works and Transportation and the Committee on Small Business.

Molinari was born on Staten Island on March 27, 1958, and attended local schools before receiving her B.A. from the State University of New York at Albany in 1980 and her M.A. in political communications from the same institution in 1982. She first worked in Washington for the Republican Governors Association and the Republican National Committee. She returned to New York City where she won election to the city council in 1985 and served there until she resigned to take her seat in the House of Representatives. As the only Republican on the city council, Molinari served as minority leader and was entitled to sit on all committees.

In her campaign for Congress, Molinari emphasized environmental issues such as water pollution, ocean dumping and protection of wetlands, all of which are of great interest to her district which includes Staten Island and a portion of Brooklyn. Molinari is also an advocate of reasonable defense spending and a strong supporter of the Navy in its construction and operation of the Stapleton homeport on Staten Island. She has worked with various issues of interest to the large veterans population in her district.

CONSTANCE A. MORELLA

(Office of Representative Morella)

United States Representative
Republican of Maryland
One Hundredth–One Hundred First Congresses
January 3, 1987–present

Soon after Constance Morella took office as a representative from Maryland's Eighth District, she won appointment to two committees crucial to her capital-area constituents. The Committee on Post Office and Civil Service oversees all legislation concerning federal workers, of whom more than 60,000 live in Morella's district. The Committee on Science,

Space, and Technology holds jurisdiction over much of the high-technology industry that has come to rival the federal government in importance for the district's economy. Morella also serves on the Select Committee on Aging.

Morella was born Constance Albanese in Somerville, Massachusetts, on February 12, 1931. She graduated with a B.A. from Boston

University in 1954. After moving to Maryland she received her M.A. in English from American University, and taught for fifteen years at Montgomery College in Rockville, Maryland. After participating in a variety of community organizations, Morella formally entered politics in 1979 as a member of the Maryland General Assembly where she served until 1987. In her initial bid for the Republican nomination to the House of Representatives she lost to former congressman Newton Steers, Jr. In 1986 Morella won the Republican nomination and defeated the Democratic candidate for the seat left open by Michael Barnes' unsuccessful Senate bid. She easily won reelection in 1988.

During her two terms in Congress, Morella has emphasized issues such as federal pay, parental leave, and health care. Among her legislative proposals is a program to encourage people to join the Peace Corps by providing college scholarships in return for three years of Peace Corps service.

MAURINE BROWN NEUBERGER

United States Senator
Democrat of Oregon
Eighty-sixth–Eighty-ninth Congresses
November 8, 1960–January 3, 1967

As a senator from Oregon, Maurine Neuberger carried on the tradition of reform legislation that she and her husband established in Oregon during the 1950s. She was born Maurine Brown in Cloverdale, Oregon, on January 9, 1907. She earned a teaching certificate at the Oregon College of Education at Monmouth in 1925 and a B.A. from the University of Oregon in 1929. She also attended graduate school at the University of California at Los Angeles. Beginning in 1932 she taught in the public schools in Milton-Freewater, Newberg, and Portland, Oregon, for twelve years. She married Richard L. Neuberger in December 1945.

In 1951 Maurine Neuberger began serving the first of two terms as a state representative from Multnomah County. (Her husband had been elected to the state senate in 1948). She chaired the House Education committee in 1953 and concentrated on consumer and education legislation. She and her husband regularly published commentaries on public issues facing the Pacific Northwest. Neuberger was a key strategist in her husband's successful 1954 attempt to win election as Oregon's first Democratic senator in forty years. She continued to work as his aide in Washington and as his liaison with constituents in Oregon.

Richard Neuberger died on March 9, 1960, two days before the filing deadline for the May primary in which he intended to seek renomination. Maurine Neuberger acceded to the appeals of numerous Oregon Democrats and declared her candidacy for both the remainder of her husband's unexpired term and for a full six-year term. Unopposed in the special election for the short term, she outdistanced four opponents in the May primary for the full term and defeated former Governor Elmo Smith in the general election.

Neuberger served on the Committee on Agriculture and Forestry, the Committee on Banking and Currency, and the Committee on Commerce, as well as on a Special Committee on Aging and a Committee on a Parliamentary Conference with Canada. She attempted to assist the industries of her state by supporting higher soybean price supports and sponsoring legislation enabling foreign ships to convey United States lumber to Puerto Rico. In 1961 she voted for redevelopment aid to areas with high unemployment and pushed to continue federal payments to states which regulated billboards along highways for two additional years. In 1962 she helped ensure that the Labor Department received funding to establish the President's Commission on the Status of Women.

Neuberger co-sponsored a measure establishing a United States travel service to encourage foreign tourism and an amendment to the Revenue Act of 1964 making it easier for taxpayers to deduct expenses for child care. In 1964 she worked with Senator Clifford Case of New Jersey in sponsoring legislation requiring Members of Congress and the executive branch to make periodic public disclosures of their financial interests. She also supported reformed immigration laws which ended the national origins quota system, advocated stronger controls on cigarette advertising and the printing of warning labels on cigarette packaging, and sponsored a bill to establish the Oregon Dunes National Seashore.

On November 1, 1965, Neuberger announced that she would not seek reelection to a second full term. Since leaving the Senate she has lectured on consumer affairs and the status of women and taught American government at Boston University, Radcliffe Institute, and Reed College. She is a resident of Portland, Oregon.

MAE ELLA HUNT NOLAN

United States Representative
Republican of California
Sixty-seventh–Sixty-eighth Congress
January 23, 1923–March 3, 1925

In the special election of January 23, 1923, Mae Ella Nolan was elected to the Sixty-eighth Congress and to the unexpired term of her husband, John I. Nolan, who had died a week following his reelection to a sixth term in Congress. With the endorsement of leading Republicans in California's Fifth District, Nolan defeated three candidates in the elec-tion and took the oath of office on February 12, 1923, during the final month of the Sixty-seventh Congress.

Mae Ella Hunt was born in San Francisco on September 20, 1886, and attended public schools, St. Vincent's Convent, and the Ayres Business College in San Francisco. She mar-ried John I. Nolan in 1913, shortly after his election to the House of Representatives on the Bull Moose ticket. When Mae Ella Nolan entered Congress she carried out her pledge to pursue the interests of her husband, particularly in regard to labor legislation and his proposal to introduce a minimum daily wage of three dollars for federal employees.

Although she ran as an independent, she received the support of the Union Labor party and the executive committee of the California Women's Republican League. Sitting as a Republican, she served on the Committee on Labor and the Committee on Woman Suffrage. In December 1923, she became the first woman to serve as chair of a committee in the House of Representatives when she took control of the Committee on Expenditures in the Post Office Department. In her one complete term in Congress, she also gained passage of several bills related to her district, including one transferring the Palace of Fine Arts from the federal government's Presidio to the city of San Francisco and another authorizing construction of a federal building. Nolan declined renomination to the Sixty-ninth Congress and returned to San Francisco. She later moved to Sacramento, where she died on July 9, 1973.

CATHERINE DORRIS NORRELL

United States Representative
Democrat of Arkansas
Eighty-seventh Congress
April 18, 1961–January 3, 1963

After more than twenty-two years as the wife of a congressman, Catherine Norrell won election to the House of Representatives from the Sixth District of Arkansas. In the special election held April 18, 1961, to fill the vacancy left by the death of her husband, William F. Norrell, Catherine Norrell defeated four other candidates for the seat from a district that was slated for absorption into two other districts in the reapportionment preceding the elections of 1962. She took the oath of office on April 25, 1961, and sat on the Committee on Post Office and Civil Service.

Like many widows running for their husband's seats, Norrell campaigned on the promise of continuing her husband's policies, and she concentrated her legislative efforts on the promotion of economic prosperity in her district. She was especially interested in protecting the area's clay, textile, and lumber industries through tariffs and other government regulation. Norrell also sponsored legislation prohibiting interstate and foreign commerce in goods imported into the United States from Cuba. In April 1962, Norrell announced she would not be a candidate for reelection.

Before her marriage to William Norrell, Catherine Dorris was a music teacher and director of the music department at Arkansas A&M College. She was born March 30, 1901, in Camden, Arkansas, and grew up in Texas, Tennessee, and Arkansas as her Baptist-preacher father moved from church to church. She attended Ouachita Baptist College in Arkadelphia and the University of Arkansas. Before her own election to the House of Representatives she worked as a staff assistant in the congressional office of her husband and served as president of the Congressional Club. Following retirement from Congress, Catherine Norrell was appointed by President Kennedy as deputy assistant secretary of state for educational and cultural affairs, and served from 1963 to 1965. From 1965 to 1969 she was director of the State Department's reception center in Honolulu, Hawaii. She lived in Monticello, Arkansas, until her death in Warren, Arkansas, on August 26, 1981.

MARY TERESA NORTON

United States Representative
Democrat of New Jersey
Sixty-ninth–Eighty-first Congresses
March 4, 1925–January 3, 1951

Mary Norton served her political apprenticeship with one of the most infamous urban machines in twentieth-century America. A protege of Jersey City's long-time mayor, Frank "I am the law" Hague, Norton, the first Democratic woman elected to the House, represented the interests of a constituency that was largely working-class and Roman Catholic. While she remained a loyal supporter of Hague and his Democratic establishment in New Jersey, she rose to become chair of the Committee on Labor in the House of Representatives and played an important role in passage of New Deal legislation related to the protection of workers.

In her earlier career, Norton worked as a stenographer and as the operator of a day nursery. She was born Mary Teresa Hopkins in Jersey City on March 7, 1875, and graduated from Jersey City High School. At the age of twenty-one she moved to New York City and attended Packard Business College. She ended her secretarial work when she married Robert Francis Norton in 1909, but following the death of her only child in 1910 she opened a day nursery in association with a local church. In her search for governmental support of the nursery she first met Jersey City's all-powerful mayor and political boss.

Hague, eager to secure newly-enfranchised women voters for the Democratic party, asked Norton to serve on the Democratic State Committee soon after the ratification of the Nineteenth Amendment. As Hudson County's representative, Norton became the first woman on the committee and served from 1921 to 1944. In 1923 Hague gained Norton a position on the county Board of Freeholders. The following year she won election to the House of Representatives from New Jersey's Twelfth District.

As a Member of Congress, the first woman to be elected from the east, Norton focused on the issues of importance to urban Democrats. She was the first representative to propose a repeal of prohibition, like other Catholics she fought to prevent the distribution of information about birth control, and she generally supported labor legislation. As a Democratic loyalist, she climbed her way up the party organization in the House. When Democrats gained a majority in the Seventy-second Congress, she became chair of the Committee on the District of Columbia and served in that capacity until 1937, gaining the nickname "Mayor of Washington" for her support of representation for the District.

Norton gave up the District Committee in the Seventy-fifth Congress to head the Committee on Labor. As chair of that committee in the latter days of the New Deal and during the Second World War, she oversaw such legislation as the Fair Labor Standards Act of 1938 and fought for equal pay for women laborers. Norton resigned from the Labor Committee in 1947 when Republicans gained control of the House and Fred Hartley became committee chairman. She also served as chair of the Committee on Memorials in the Seventy-seventh Congress and of the Committee on House Administration in the Eighty-first Congress.

Norton declined to run for reelection in 1950 but remained in Washington to work as a consultant for the Department of Labor in 1951 and 1952. She died in Greenwich, Connecticut, on August 2, 1959.

MARY ROSE OAKAR

United States Representative
Democrat of Ohio
Ninety-fifth–One Hundred First Congresses
January 3, 1977–present

Mary Rose Oakar, in seven terms in Congress, has established a place for herself in the internal operation of the House of Representatives while pursuing legislative matters of interest to her and her constituents. Starting as a member of the Democratic whip's organization, she worked her way to the position of vice chair of the Democratic Caucus in the Ninety-ninth and One-Hundredth Congresses. A member of the Committee on House Administration since the Ninety-eighth Congress, Oakar serves as chair of the Subcommittee on Personnel and Police which oversees an important part of the internal business of the House.

Oakar also serves on the Committee on Banking, Finance and Urban Affairs (where she is chair of the Subcommittee on Economic Stabilization), the Committee on Post Office and Civil Service, and the Select Committee on Aging. These assignments provide a forum for her to pursue such issues as economic redevelopment of older industrial areas like her district, equal and comparable pay for women in the workforce, and benefits for congressional employees.

The Cleveland native spent almost her entire life in that Ohio city prior to her election to Congress. She was born March 5, 1940, and graduated from Ursuline College in 1962 with a B.A. and from John Carroll University with a Masters in 1966. She also studied at the Royal Academy of Dramatic Arts in London, Westham Adult College in England, and at Columbia University in New York City. Oakar taught at a high school and community college in Cleveland from 1963 to 1975.

From 1973 to 1976 Oakar served as a member of the Cleveland City Council where she won broad public support. In 1976 she entered the Democratic primary for an open House seat in Ohio's Twentieth District and defeated eleven other candidates before going on to win the general election. She since has enjoyed easy reelection.

CAROLINE LOVE GOODWIN O'DAY

(U.S. House of Representatives)

United States Representative
Democrat of New York
Seventy-fourth–Seventy-seventh Congresses
January 3, 1935–January 3, 1943

Caroline Goodwin was born on June 22, 1875, on her grandfather's plantation in Perry, Georgia. She attended private schools and was graduated from Lucy Cobb Institute in Athens, Georgia. For eight years she studied art in Paris, Munich, and Holland and achieved success as a painter, magazine illustrator, and costume designer. In 1902 she married oil company executive Daniel T. O'Day, whom she met in Europe.

While living in New York City O'Day became interested in improving the lives of inner city residents and served on the board of directors of Lillian Wald's Henry Street Settlement on the lower East Side. She was active in the Women's International League for Peace and Freedom, an offshoot of the National Woman's Party, and was a supporter of organized labor. She occasionally turned her Rye, New York, estate over to trade unions for their conferences and meetings. She belonged to a commission to establish a minimum wage scale for laundry workers and served as a commissioner of the state board of social welfare from 1923 to 1934. O'Day served as president of the Rye, New York, school board and became active in the Democratic politics of Westchester County shortly after ratification of the Nineteenth Amendment. In 1923 she became associate chair of the New York State Democratic committee and directed its women's division, holding these posts until her death. During the 1920s she established friendships and alliances with Democratic party officials throughout New York, including Eleanor Roosevelt, who was just beginning to emerge as a public figure in her own right. Together they led delegations of women to Albany to urge legislative approval of the programs of Governor Alfred E. Smith. She worked for Smith's presidential campaign of 1928 and the Roosevelt presidential campaign of 1932. After Roosevelt's inauguration, she was appointed state director of the National Recovery Administration.

In 1934 O'Day ran for New York's at-large seat in the House of Representatives. Aided by support from the Roosevelt administration and personal campaign appearances by the First Lady, O'Day topped a slate of eleven candidates. She served on the Committee on Immigration and Naturalization and the Committee on Insular Affairs and chaired the Committee on Election of President, Vice President, and Representatives in Congress from 1937 to 1943. While in Congress she continued to support pro-labor legislation and was a warm friend of the New Deal. She helped attach a child labor amendment to the 1936 Walsh-Healey Act, which set employment standards for government contractors, and to the 1938 Fair Labor Standards Act, which fixed minimum ages for employment. As a pacifist she opposed modification of the Neutrality Act of 1939 to authorize arms sales to nations at war with Nazi Germany and voted against the 1940 Selective Training and Service Act. She chaired the committee which sponsored singer Marian Anderson's historic 1939 concert at the Lincoln Memorial.

Suffering from health problems as the result of a fall in the summer of 1942, O'Day declined to run for renomination for a fifth term and died January 4, 1943, the day following the end of her congressional service.

PEARL PEDEN OLDFIELD

(U.S. House of Representatives)

United States Representative
Democrat of Arkansas
Seventieth–Seventy-first Congress
January 11, 1929–March 3, 1931

Pearl Oldfield represented the Second District of Arkansas at a time when natural disaster and economic depression threatened the livelihood and welfare of her rural constituents. During her service of slightly more than one term, she sponsored legislation to continue federal aid for the rehabilitation of farmland damaged by the Mississippi River floods of 1927. In January 1931 she asked her House colleagues to approve a $15 million food appropriation to alleviate malnutrition in drought-affected areas such as her own district where Red Cross efforts were inadequate to meet the demand for food. Oldfield also sponsored legislation to authorize the Arkansas Highway Commission to construct free bridges across the Black and White Rivers in the Second District.

On January 9, 1929, Pearl Oldfield was elected without opposition to fill the vacancy in the Seventieth Congress left by the death of her husband and ten-term representative, William A. Oldfield. On the same day, Pearl Oldfield defeated independent candidate R.W. Tucker for election to the Seventy-first Congress to which her husband had won reelection shortly before his death on November 19, 1928. Pearl Oldfield was sworn in on January 11, 1929, and served on the Committee on Coinage, Weights and Measures, the Committee on Expenditures in the Executive Departments, and the Committee on Public Buildings and Grounds. In May 1929, she announced that she would not be a candidate for reelection to the Seventy-second Congress.

Pearl Peden was born in Cotton Plant, Arkansas, on December 2, 1876, and attended Arkansas College in Batesville. She died in Washington, D.C., on April 12, 1962.

RUTH BRYAN OWEN

(U.S. House of Representatives)

United States Representative
Democrat of Florida
Seventy-first–Seventy-second Congresses
March 4, 1929–March 3, 1933

Daughter of "The Peerless Leader," three-time presidential nominee William Jennings Bryan, Ruth Bryan Owen dedicated herself to the twin causes of domestic reform and international peace. She was born in Jacksonville, Illinois, on October 2, 1885, and moved with her family to Lincoln, Nebraska, two years later. After her father's election to the House of Representatives in 1890, she attended public schools in Washington, D.C., and the Monticello Female Academy in Godfrey, Illinois, before entering the University of Nebraska at Lincoln in 1901.

Bryan left college to marry William Homer Leavitt in October 1903 and served as her father's traveling secretary during his third presidential campaign in 1908. She divorced Leavitt the following year and in 1910 married Major Reginald Owen of the Royal (British) Engineers. She accompanied her husband to his posts in Jamaica, the West Indies, and London. A member of the executive committee of the American Women's War Relief Fund in London, Owen served as a war nurse in the Voluntary Aid Detachment during the Egypt-Palestine campaign of 1915–1918.

In 1919 the Owen family returned to the United States and settled in Miami, Florida. During the next ten years, Ruth Bryan Owen was a Chautauqua lecturer and served on the faculty of the University of Miami from 1926 to 1928. She was vice chair of the board of regents from 1925 to 1928.

In a state that had refused to ratify the Nineteenth Amendment, Owen entered Florida politics and in 1926 narrowly lost the Democratic primary bid to represent the Fourth District. She was widowed the next year. In 1928 she defeated seven-term incumbent William J. Sears in the primary for the Fourth District nomination. During the general election campaign she kept her distance from the her party's presidential nominee, Al Smith, and defeated Republican William C. Lawson. Lawson contested her election, charging that Owen had lost her American citizenship upon her marriage to an alien and was ineligible for election to Congress because she had not recovered it under the provisions of the 1922 Cable Act until 1925. Owen offered a persuasive and successful defense of her eligibility and exposed the Cable Act's deficiencies before House Committee on Elections No. 1.

Owen became a member of the Seventy-first Congress on March 4, 1929, and served on the Foreign Affairs Committee. She astonished many observers who recalled her father's opposition to tariffs by voting in favor of the 1930 Smoot-Hawley Tariff which raised duties on imports. Her farsighted proposals included designation of the Florida Everglades as a national park and the establishment of a cabinet-level department to oversee the health and welfare of families and children.

After winning reelection to the Seventy-second Congress, Owen in 1932 lost another bid for renomination to James M. Wilcox, who had attacked her stand in favor of Prohibition. During the second, or "lame duck" session of the Seventy-second Congress, Owen voted to repeal the Eighteenth Amendment, explaining that her views had not altered but that she was giving voice to the expressed will of her constituents.

In April 1933 President Roosevelt appointed Owen Minister to Denmark. She resigned in August 1936, shortly after her marriage to Captain Borge Rohde of the Danish Royal Guards. Because her marriage meant that she was now a citizen of both Denmark and the United States, she was unable to continue at her diplomatic assignment and spent the summer and fall campaigning for Roosevelt's reelection.

Owen served on the Advisory Board of the Federal Reformatory for Women from 1938 until 1954 and was an alternate delegate to the 1949 United Nations General Assembly. She resided in Ossining, New York, and engaged in literary work, lecturing, and various activities promoting the United Nations. While in Copenhagen to accept a decoration awarded by King Frederick IX, she died on July 26, 1954.

ELIZABETH J. PATTERSON

(Office of Representative Patterson)

United States Representative
Democrat of South Carolina
One Hundredth–One Hundred First Congresses
January 3, 1987–present

Elizabeth Patterson's election to Congress followed a lifetime of involvement with government and politics. Born Elizabeth Johnston in Columbia, South Carolina, on November 18, 1939, she graduated from Columbia College in 1961 and attended graduate school at the University of South Carolina the following year. As a young girl she worked in

the Senate campaigns of her father, Olin D. Johnston, a former governor of South Carolina and senator from that state from 1945 to 1965.

Following college, Liz Patterson worked as a recruiting officer for the Peace Corps and VISTA, as Head Start coordinator for the South Carolina Office of Economic Opportunity, and as a staff assistant for South Carolina Representative James R. Mann. She first held political office when she served on the Spartanburg County Council in 1975 and 1976. Patterson was a member of the South Carolina Senate from 1979 to 1987.

Patterson declared her candidacy for the House seat in South Carolina's Fourth District in 1986 when four-term Republican Representative Carroll Campbell, Jr. declined renomination in order to run for governor. Patterson defeated the Republican nominee and won reelection in 1988 despite the district's overwhelming Republican vote in that year's presidential contest. Patterson sits on the Committee on Veterans' Affairs, the Committee on Banking, Finance and Urban Affairs, and the Select Committee on Hunger.

NANCY PELOSI

(Office of Representative Pelosi)

United States Representative
Democrat of California
One Hundredth–One Hundred First Congresses
June 2, 1987–present

Nancy Pelosi entered the House of Representatives after winning a special election on June 2, 1987, to fill the vacancy left by the death of Sala Burton. Raised in a politically prominent family in Maryland and long active in the Democratic organization in California, Pelosi was thoroughly familiar with politics despite no previous experience in elective office.

Pelosi was born in Baltimore on March 26, 1940, the daughter of Thomas D'Alesandro, Jr., who served in the House of Representatives from 1939 to 1947 and later was mayor of Baltimore. Pelosi's brother also served as mayor of their native city. After growing up in Baltimore, she received her undergraduate degree from Trinity College in Washington, D.C., in 1962.

Following her move to San Francisco, Pelosi became involved in the Democratic Party and served as chair of the California State Democratic Party from 1981 to 1983, during which time she helped secure San Francisco as the site of the national convention in 1984. She also served as finance chair of the Democratic Senatorial Campaign Committee in 1986 when the party regained a majority in the U.S. Senate.

Shortly before Sala Burton's death in January of 1987, she endorsed Pelosi as her successor. With the support of Burton's backers and her knowledge of the state party organization, Pelosi won a close race in the special primary and easily won the runoff election. As a member of the House, Pelosi serves on the Committee on Banking, Finance and Urban Affairs and the Committee on Government Operations. She has sponsored a wide variety of legislation designed to increase the government's role in response to every dimension of the AIDS epidemic. She also has worked to provide more housing for low- and moderate-income communities.

SHIRLEY NEIL PETTIS

(U.S. House of Representatives)

United States Representative
Republican of California
Ninety-fourth–Ninety-fifth Congresses
April 29, 1975–January 3, 1979

Shirley Pettis worked as a journalist and assisted her husband in the operation of their ranch before she succeeded to his seat in the House of Representatives. She was elected in a special election in California's Thirty-seventh District on April 29, 1975, to fill the vacancy left when Jerry L. Pettis was killed in a private airplane crash. She secured over 60 percent of the vote against three other candidates. After taking the oath of office on May 6, she was appointed to the Committee on Interior and Insular Affairs. She won reelection to a full term in the Ninety-fifth Congress and served on the Committee on Education and Labor and the Committee on International Relations.

Shirley Neil McCumber was born in Mountain View, California, on July 12, 1924. She attended schools in Berkeley, California, and Berrien Springs, Michigan. She studied at Andrews University in Berrien Springs and at the University of California at Berkeley. Pettis was a founder and manager of the Audio-Digest Foundation and following her husband's election to Congress in 1966, she wrote a newspaper column for the *San Bernardino Sun-Telegram.*

In her first term in the House of Representatives, Pettis used her seat on Interior and Insular Affairs to gain legislation protecting desert lands in her district. She secured wilderness status for almost a half million acres in the Joshua Tree National Monument and established the California Desert Conservation area. Pettis declined to run for renomination in 1978. She is a resident of Los Angeles.

GRACIE BOWERS PFOST

(U.S. House of Representatives)

United States Representative
Democrat of Idaho
Eighty-third–Eighty-seventh Congresses
January 3, 1953–January 3, 1963

Gracie Pfost fought so tenaciously for federal development of the Hell's Canyon branch of the Snake River that she won the sobriquet "Hell's Belle." She was born in Harrison, Arkansas, on March 12, 1906. In 1911 she moved with her parents to a farm in Idaho's Boise Valley. Pfost attended public schools and graduated from Link's Business College and

Secretarial School in Boise in 1929. She was a chemist for a milk products company for two years. Between 1929 and 1939 Pfost served as deputy county clerk, auditor, and recorder of Canyon County, Idaho. She was treasurer of Canyon County from 1941 to 1951. During 1951 and 1952 she owned and operated a real estate business in Nampa, Idaho. She was a delegate to every Democratic National Convention from 1944 to 1960.

Pfost ran for the House of Representatives from Idaho's First District in 1950 but lost to incumbent John T. Wood by 783 votes out of almost 83,000 cast. In a rematch two years later her campaign slogan was designed to let the electorate know how to pronounce her last name: "Tie Your Vote to a Solid Post-Gracie Pfost for Congress." She defeated Wood by 591 votes. In December 1952 Wood asked the House Committee on Elections to conduct a recount, but his request was rejected because the Committee was due to lapse at the end of the Eighty-second Congress.

Pfost served on the Committee on Public Works, the Committee on Post Office and Civil Service, and the Committee on Interior and Insular Affairs where she chaired the public lands subcommittee. She first attracted national attention as a member of the Select Committee to Investigate Tax-exempt Foundations and Comparable Organizations which examined such philanthropic organizations as the Ford Foundation and the Fund for the Republic to determine if funds were granted for un-American activities. On May 24, 1954, Pfost and Wayne Hays of Ohio walked out of the hearings and accused the committee of permitting unreliable testimony against foundation employees and failing to require witnesses to submit prepared statements or digests of testimony prior to their appearances.

As a result of their withdrawal, the Committee voted in July to end its hearings. Pfost dissented from the final Committee report which concluded that several foundations had unwittingly subsidized subversive ventures.

Throughout the 1950s the Snake River dam was the divisive issue in the politics of the Northwest, separating advocates of regional development through low-cost public power from those opposed to any governmental competition with private enterprise. Pfost protested bitterly in August 1955 when the Federal Power Commission granted the Idaho Power Company a license to construct the dams, charging that the Eisenhower administration was dominated by big business. She suffered a final defeat in July 1957 when the Interior and Insular Affairs Committee voted to discard her bill, first proposed in April 1953, to build the Snake River power and flood control dams with federal money.

In 1962 Pfost declined to run for reelection in order to seek the Democratic nomination for the United States Senate seat to which Republican Len B. Jordan had been appointed following the death of Senator Henry Dworshak. She was nominated by the Democratic state central committee in August but lost to Jordan in the general election.

Pfost worked for the Federal Housing Administration as a Special Assistant for Elderly Housing from June 1963 until her death in Baltimore on August 11, 1965.

ELIZA JANE PRATT

United States Representative
Democrat of North Carolina
Seventy-ninth Congress
May 25, 1946–January 3, 1947

More than twenty years before her election to the House of Representatives, Eliza Jane Pratt went to Capitol Hill to work as a staff assistant. From 1924 to 1946 she served as administrative assistant to a succession of congressmen from North Carolina's Eighth District. When Representative William O. Burgin died in April 1946, the North Carolina Democratic executive committee nominated her for the special election to succeed the Member for whom she had worked. Following a five-week campaign in which she paid all her own expenses, Pratt won a lop-sided victory over Republican candidate H. Frank Hulin on May 25, 1946.

Pratt took the oath of office on June 3, 1946, and was appointed to the Committee on Pensions, the Committee on Territories, and the Committee on Flood Control. Following Congress's adjournment on August 2, she declined to run for reelection. Pratt remained in Washington working for the Office of Alien Property from 1947 to 1951, the Department of Agriculture from 1951 to 1954, and the Library of Congress from 1954 to 1956. She returned to Capitol Hill to work as secretary to Eighth District Representative Alvin P. Kitchin from 1957 to 1962.

Before her Washington career, Pratt worked as a newspaper editor in Troy, North Carolina. She was born in Morven, North Carolina, on March 5, 1902, and attended schools there and in Raeford, North Carolina. She later enrolled at Queens College in Charlotte. Pratt returned to her native state to work for the North Carolina Telephone Company and lived in Wadesboro until her death in Charlotte on May 13, 1981.

RUTH SEARS BAKER PRATT

United States Representative
Republican of New York
Seventy-first–Seventy-second Congresses
March 4, 1929–March 3, 1933

Ruth Pratt's background of family wealth, social position, commitment to civic causes and familiarity with big-city politics proved to be solid assets when she was elected in 1928 as a Republican from Manhattan's "Silk Stocking" district. The daughter of a cotton manufacturer, she was born in Ware, Massachusetts, on August 24, 1877, and attended

Dana Hall in Wellesley, Massachusetts, and Wellesley College. She moved to Greenwich, Connecticut, in 1894 and to New York City in 1904 after her marriage to John T. Pratt, son of an oil company executive.

During World War I Ruth Pratt chaired the Second Federal Reserve District's Woman's Liberty Loan Committee. In 1918 she was appointed vice chair of the Republican National Ways and Means Committee and worked for Herbert Hoover's presidential nomination in 1920. In January 1924 Pratt was elected associate leader of the Fifteenth Assembly District, which would remain her political base for the next decade. She was a member of the Republican National Committee from 1929 to 1943.

Campaigning against the administration of Mayor John F. Hylan and as a champion of a non-partisan parks commission, Pratt in November 1925 became the first woman elected to the New York City Board of Aldermen. She often found herself at odds with Hylan's successor, James J. Walker. In 1928 she introduced legislation calling for a referendum to revise the city charter and introduced measures to authorize construction of the Triborough Bridge and tunnels under the East River.

In September 1928 Pratt defeated Democrat Phillip Berolzheimer to win election to the House of Representatives from New York's Seventeenth District. Shortly after her arrival in Washington she leased "Evermay," an 18th-century Georgian manor in Georgetown, and was sworn in when the Seventy-first Congress convened on April 15, 1929. During her four years in the House Pratt served on the Committee on Education, the Committee on Banking and Currency, and the Committee on the Library. In her first House speech she criticized a proviso of the Hawley tariff bill that raised the duty on sugar, arguing that the increase would raise the cost of sugar and would not be used to improve the wages and conditions of sugar workers.

In January 1930 Pratt introduced a bill for a $75,000 annual appropriation to acquire and publish books for the blind. She favored repeal of the Eighteenth Amendment (Prohibition) and praised President Hoover for his reliance on private funding to alleviate unemployment.

In her reelection bid of 1930 Pratt faced a socialist candidate, the controversial journalist Heywood Broun. She feared his candidacy would increase the likelihood of a victory for Tammany Hall's candidate, City Magistrate Louis B. Brodsky, but she managed to win by 695 votes.

A devoted supporter of Hoover, Pratt seconded his renomination at the 1932 Republican convention. In the September primary she weathered charges from opponents that she had abused the franking privilege by mailing seventy thousand pamphlets to her district describing her achievements, as well as a reprint of a Walter Lippmann column praising the Republican Party's position on Prohibition. In the general election she lost to Theodore A. Peyser.

Pratt served as chair of the Fine Arts Foundation, a forerunner of the National Endowment for the Humanities, and was appointed to the advisory committee of the Republican Builders, a group formed to renew the party after the defeats of 1932 and 1934. She continued to live in New York City and was president of the Women's National Republican Club from 1943 to 1946. She died in Glen Cove, New York, on August 23, 1965.

GLADYS PYLE

(U.S. House of Representatives)

United States Senator
Republican of South Dakota
Seventy-fifth Congress
November 9, 1938–January 3, 1939

Gladys Pyle came to Washington in 1938 as the first Republican woman elected to the Senate, but she never was sworn in as a member of that body. The Senate adjourned in June 1938, five months before Pyle's victory in the special election of November 9, 1938, held to fill the vacancy caused by the death of Senator Peter Norbeck. She easily defeated state legislator John T. McCullen for the right to serve the final weeks of Norbeck's term. In her two months as a senator, Pyle worked with governmental agencies responsible for programs affecting South Dakota and participated in national Republican Party meetings.

The disappointing Senate career of Pyle stood in contrast to her long and influential participation in the government of her native South Dakota. She was born in Huron on October 4, 1890, and attended schools in Miller, Wessington, and Huron. Pyle graduated from Huron College and entered graduate work at the American Conservatory of Music and the University of Chicago. She returned to South Dakota to work as a high school teacher and principal.

The daughter of one of the state's leading suffragists, Pyle showed an early interest in politics and won election as the first woman member of the state legislature in 1922. After four years service as a state representative, she served four years as secretary of state. In 1930 she was an unsuccessful candidate for governor. Before her election to the Senate, Pyle worked in the life insurance business.

Pyle continued in public life, serving on the state board of charities and corrections from 1943 to 1957, and renewed her insurance business from 1950 to 1986. At the Republican National Convention of 1940, she nominated South Dakota's favorite-son presidential candidate, Governor Harlan J. Bushfield. Pyle died in Huron on March 14, 1989.

JEANNETTE RANKIN

United States Representative
Republican of Montana
Sixty-fifth and Seventy-seventh Congresses
March 4, 1917–March 3, 1919,
January 3, 1941–January 3, 1943

The first woman to serve in Congress entered politics through her participation in the campaign for woman suffrage and while in office worked to secure a constitutional amendment guaranteeing women the right to vote. Jeannette Rankin served two terms, separated by more than twenty years, in the House of Representatives during a lengthy career devoted more to contemporary reform movements than to institutional politics. A devoted advocate of the mid-twentieth century peace movement, Rankin was the only Member of Congress who voted against United States' entry into both World Wars.

Jeannette Pickering Rankin was born on a ranch near Missoula, Montana, on June 11, 1880. After graduation from the University of Montana in 1902, she worked in odd jobs before enrolling at the New York School of Philanthropy in 1908. Frustrated in her social work in Montana and Washington, Rankin enrolled at the University of Washington for further study in 1909 and simultaneously joined the state's woman suffrage movement in time to enjoy its success one year later. She continued to work for suffrage in other states and in 1913 became field secretary for the National American Woman Suffrage Association.

Montana's approval of woman suffrage in 1914 created the opportunity for Rankin to run for public office in her home state. In 1916, with her brother Wellington as a campaign manager, she won the Republican primary for the nomination for one of Montana's two at-large seats in the House of Representative and carried the general election in November.

The attention devoted to the swearing in of the first woman elected to the House of Representatives was soon overshadowed by President Wilson's call for a war resolution on the evening Congress convened in April 1917. Aware of the impending vote, rival women's political groups tried to persuade Rankin that her vote would speak for all women. Carrie Chapman Catt of the National American Woman Suffrage Association feared a vote against war would brand suffragists as unpatriotic while Alice Paul of the Woman's Party thought women in politics should speak for peace. Rankin, who had not previously identified herself as a pacifist, announced that she could not vote for war and in joining the fifty-six other Members who voted against the war resolution embarked on the cause that would be at the center of her life until her death more than a half century later. Rankin devoted the remainder of her term to legislation related to her earlier reform efforts. She was ranking minority member on the special committee formed to draft a woman suffrage amendment to the Constitution, although the Senate's failure to pass the measure delayed that achievement until the succeeding Con-

gress. Rankin also sponsored a bill to establish a program of women's health education that later passed as the Sheppard-Towner Act. When the Industrial Workers of the World petitioned the federal government to intervene in the miners conflict with Anaconda Copper Company, Rankin agreed to present their demand to governmental officials.

The division of Montana into two distinct congressional districts made it impossible for Rankin to run a state-wide campaign for reelection and convinced her to run instead for the Senate. She lost the Republican primary in Montana and in November of 1918 ran on the ticket of a newly-established reform coalition, the National Party. For twenty years following her retirement from Congress in 1919 Rankin was actively involved in a variety of pacifist organizations such as the Women's International League for Peace and Freedom. She served also as field representative for the National Council for the Prevention of War. In between her many travels she lived in rural Georgia and largely ignored electoral and party politics except for one ill-fated effort to convince her neighbors to vote against their popular congressman and powerful chairman of the Committee on Naval Affairs, Carl Vinson.

In 1940 Rankin returned to Montana where she maintained her legal residence and ran for Congress on an isolationist platform as the Republican candidate. She defeated a New-Deal Democrat, Jerry O'Connell, and returned to the House of Representatives for the opening of the Seventy-seventh Congress on January 3, 1941. When Congress faced another war resolution on December 8, Rankin was unable to get Speaker Rayburn's permission to address the House and to a chorus of jeers from the gallery was the lone Member of either house to vote against war with Japan. With no chance of reelection, Rankin returned to Montana and divided her time between there and Georgia.

In the years following the war, Rankin made various trips to India to study the pacifism of Gandhi and others. She briefly reentered public life in the late 1960s when a coalition of women organized themselves as the

Jeannette Rankin Brigade and marched on Washington in protest of the war in Vietnam. Rankin considered another run for Congress in 1968, at the age of eighty-eight, but poor health prevented her. She died in Carmel, California, on May 18, 1973.

LOUISE GOFF REECE

(U.S. House of Representatives)

United States Representative
Republican of Tennessee
Eighty-seventh Congress
May 16, 1961–January 3, 1963

After the First District Republican Committee endorsed Louise Reece as a candidate to succeed to her husband's House seat, she won the nomination from the district convention and defeated Democrat William Faw in the special election of May 16, 1961. She went on to complete the term of B. Carroll Reece, who died in office. She followed in the service not only of her husband but of her father, Guy Goff, a United States senator from West Virginia, and her grandfather, Nathan Goff, a senator and representative also from West Virginia.

Louise Goff was born in Milwaukee, Wisconsin, on November 6, 1898, and was educated at private schools in Milwaukee and Miss

Spence's School in New York City. After marrying Representative Carroll Reece and moving to Johnson City, Tennessee, she became involved in various business activities. She also regularly campaigned with her husband during his twelve terms in Congress.

Reece took the oath of office on May 23, 1961, and served on the Committee on Public Works. In an effort to protect her district's glass industry, she joined with West Virginia Representative Cleveland Bailey in urging President Kennedy to restore tariff rates on certain glass products. She joined the other Republicans on the Public Works Committee in issuing a report in opposition to the Public Works Acceleration and Coordination Act that they thought would needlessly increase federal spending and overburden the bureaucracy. In a special order marking the forty-fifth anniversary of the Nineteenth Amendment guaranteeing women the right to vote, Reece recalled the role of Tennessee in providing the final vote for ratification.

Citing the need to elect a younger Member from the district, Reece announced in January 1962 that she would not be a candidate for reelection. She returned to her business interests in Tennessee and West Virginia. On May 14, 1970, she died in Johnson City, Tennessee.

CHARLOTTE THOMPSON REID

(U.S. House of Representatives)

United States Representative
Republican of Illinois
Eighty-eighth–Ninety-second Congresses
January 3, 1963–October 7, 1971

Charlotte Reid's career in the broadcasting industry began when she was a radio vocalist in the 1930s and was capped with her appointment as a member of the Federal Communications Commission nearly thirty years later. In between those years she served as a Republican representative in Congress. She was born Charlotte Leota Thompson on September 27, 1913, in Kankakee, Illinois. She moved with her family to Aurora, Illinois, and graduated from East Aurora High School in 1930. After two years of study at Illinois College in Jacksonville she devoted full time to her professional singing career. Beginning in 1936 she was associated with NBC's Chicago-based

"Don McNeill's Breakfast Club," singing under the name of Annette King.

Thompson married Aurora attorney Frank R. Reid in January 1938 and became active in civic, community, and political affairs in the Aurora area. Her husband died in August 1962 while campaigning as the Republican candidate for the House seat from Illinois' Fifteenth District. The District's Republican county chairmen selected Charlotte Reid to replace his candidacy and she defeated the Democratic nominee, Stanley H. Cowan, with over 60 percent of the vote.

After entering the Eighty-eighth Congress, Reid served on the Committee on Interior and Insular Affairs. In later terms she served on the Committee on Appropriations, the Committee on Public Works, and the Committee on Standards of Official Conduct. She sought to protect the economic needs of her district through agricultural price supports. At the same time she supported construction of a National Cultural Center in Washington, D.C., but maintained that it should be funded through individual contributions rather than federal appropriations.

During the Eighty-eighth Congress Reid introduced a constitutional amendment to enable public school students to engage in noncompulsory prayer. As a critic of an expanded federal bureaucracy, she opposed many of the social programs of President Lyndon Johnson's Great Society. At the same time she endorsed improved safety standards for motor vehicles, the 1968 Omnibus Crime Control and Safe Streets Act, a measure to outlaw mail-order and out-of-state sales of rifles, and a "Truth in Lending" law requiring the disclosure of annual percentage costs of loans and installment plans. She supported the proposed Equal Rights Amendment to the Constitution.

In the face of growing opposition to American participation in the Vietnam War, Reid remained a steadfast supporter of the military policies of Presidents Johnson and Nixon. She voted for a 1968 amendment to a higher education bill that denied federal loans to students who joined in demonstrations against the war, and she opposed the Cooper-Church amendment designed to limit American involvement with the war in Southeast Asia.

In July 1971 President Nixon nominated Reid for a seven-year term on the Federal Communications Commission, but requested her to remain in the House during the consideration of the administration's legislative program. Reid was unanimously confirmed by the Senate later in July and she resigned from the House on October 7. She served on the FCC until July 1976. She was a member of the President's Task Force on International Private Enterprise from 1983 to 1985, and has been a member of the Hoover Institution's Board of Overseers since 1984. She is a resident of Aurora, Illinois.

CORRINE BOYD RILEY

United States Representative
Democrat of South Carolina
Eighty-seventh Congress
April 10, 1962–January 3, 1963

Corrine Riley succeeded to the seat of her late husband without any campaign appearances prior to the special election of April 10, 1962. After the death of John Jacob Riley on January 1, 1962, both the Democratic and Republican national committeemen from South Carolina urged his widow to run for the unexpired term of the Second District representative. Although she initially resisted, she announced her candidacy in mid-January and in the primary of February 13 she defeated Martha T. Fitzgerald, an eleven-term member of the South Carolina House of Representatives. Riley, who promised only to pursue the conservative agenda of her husband, was unopposed in the April special election.

After taking the oath of office on April 12, 1962, Riley was assigned a seat on the Committee on Science and Astronautics after resisting earlier offers of the Committee on Education and Labor or the Committee on Post Office and Civil Services. In her eight-month term, Riley introduced a bill authorizing the General Services Administration to transfer surplus property to the Aiken, South Carolina, Historical Society for use as a historical monument. She also spoke in favor of legislation authorizing the Federal Communications Commission to require television sets to be equipped with both ultra and very high frequency channels; a proposal she hoped would benefit an educational television station operating in her district.

Born Corrine Boyd in Piedmont, South Carolina, on July 4, 1893, she graduated from Converse College in Spartanburg in 1915. She taught high school from 1915 to 1937 and served as a field representative for the South Carolina textbook commission from 1938 to 1942. During the Second World War, Riley worked for the Civilian Personnel Office at Shaw Air Force Base in Sumter, South Carolina. After her brief House service she returned to Sumter where she died on April 12, 1979.

ALICE MARY ROBERTSON

United States Representative
Republican of Oklahoma
Sixty-seventh Congress
March 4, 1921–March 3, 1923

In 1920, a year when Republicans gained more than sixty seats in the House of Representatives, Alice Mary Robertson became the second woman elected to the House when she defeated the three-term incumbent Democrat, William Wirt Hastings, in Oklahoma's Second District. At the age of sixty-seven Robertson had a diverse career behind her. She was born January 2, 1854, at the Tullahassee Mission of the Creek Nation in Indian Territory (now Oklahoma). Taught by her missionary parents, she went on to attend Elmira College in New York. From 1873 to 1879 she worked as the first woman clerk in the Office of Indian Affairs in Washington. Robertson later taught at a school in the Indian Territory, at the

217

Indian school in Carlisle, Pennsylvania, and at a mission she founded among the Creek nation. She held various administrative and teaching posts with Henry Kendall College (now the University of Tulsa). From 1905 to 1913 she was postmaster of Muskogee, Oklahoma. Later she operated a dairy farm and cafeteria in Muskogee.

As a candidate for Congress in the first election following ratification of the Nineteenth Amendment, Robertson dissociated herself from suffragists and other women's rights advocates. She remained a foe of such organizations as the League of Women Voters and the National Women's Party. In the House, she refused to support legislation central to the political agenda of many women. In 1921 she spoke out against the Sheppard-Towner bill which provided the Labor Department's Children's Bureau with $1 million annually to promote maternity and infant care. Robertson's opposition to what she saw as a bureaucratic intrusion on personal rights provoked condemnation from women's political groups and such organizations as the Daughters of the American Revolution.

In the Sixty-seventh Congress, Robertson served on the Committee on Expenditures in the Interior Department, the Committee on Indian Affairs, and the Committee on Woman Suffrage. During the First World War, Robertson had established a canteen for servicemen in Muskogee, but as a representative she voted against the Soldiers' Bonus Bill. In support of servicemen, she won approval for an amendment increasing the subsistence rate and rent money for Army and Navy nurses. Robertson opposed United States entry into the League of Nations and challenged Representative Meyer London of New York when he urged the release of Eugene Debs from prison.

On June 20, 1921, during a roll call vote on funding for a United States delegation to the centennial celebrations of Peru's independence, Robertson became the first woman to preside over a session of the House of Representatives. Her first term in Congress, however, was also to be the last for the outspoken Robertson. In a rematch with William W. Hastings in 1922, Robertson lost her seat. Failing to receive an appointment in Indian affairs in the Harding administration, Robertson returned to Oklahoma where she worked in the Veterans' Hospital in Muskogee, served as a correspondent, and worked for the Oklahoma Historical Society. She died in Muskogee on July 1, 1931.

EDITH NOURSE ROGERS

United States Representative
Republican of Massachusetts
Sixty-ninth–Eighty-sixth Congresses
June 30, 1925–September 10, 1960

The longest-serving woman in the history of Congress, like so many other women in Congress, began her career in the House of Representatives as the replacement for her husband who had died in office. After winning the Republican primary earlier in the month, Edith Nourse Rogers went on to win the special election of June 30, 1925, held to fill the va-

cancy left when Fifth District Representative John Jacob Rogers died in March of 1925. Edith Rogers won another seventeen elections before her death in office in 1960.

Edith Nourse was born in Saco, Maine, on March 19, 1881. Her wealthy family offered her a privileged education of private tutors, boarding school, and attendance at Madame

Julien's finishing school outside of Paris. She moved with her family in 1895 to Lowell, Massachusetts, where her father became an agent for a textile mill. There Edith Nourse entered society and in 1907 married John Jacob Rogers who opened up a law practice in the city. In 1912 he won election to the first of seven terms in the House of Representatives. Edith Rogers accompanied her husband to Washington where they became noted for their entertainments.

During the First World War Edith Rogers traveled to Europe inspecting field hospitals with the Women's Overseas Service and returned to work as a Red Cross volunteer in Washington. This activity continued after the war when she devoted much of her time to the problems of veterans. Presidents Harding, Coolidge and Hoover offered her successive appointments as an assistant for programs dealing with disabled veterans.

Rogers' volunteer service halted when her husband died and she agreed to stand for election to his House seat. Rogers applied her experience with veterans' issues to her work with the Committee on World War Veterans Legislation which she joined in her first term in Congress. She served on the committee and its successor, Veterans' Affairs, throughout her congressional career and was chair of Veterans' Affairs in the Eightieth and Eighty-third Congresses. Among her legislative achievements in this area were the bill to establish the Women's Army Corps and sponsorship of the G.I. Bill, the Korean Veterans' Benefits bill, and the bill establishing a Nurses Corps in the Veterans' Administration.

Concern with veterans' issues increased Rogers' interest in foreign policy. By the mid-1930s she was warning her colleagues of the dangers presented by Hitler's Germany, and she broke with her fellow Republicans in 1937 by voting against the Neutrality Act and in 1940 by voting for the Selective Service Act. She supported the investigations of the Committee on Un-American Activities and Senator McCarthy. Rogers remained a popular representative who frequently visited her district and carefully defended the textile industry of the region. Rogers intended to run for a nineteenth term at the age of seventy-nine in 1960, but after checking into a Boston hospital under an assumed name, she died three days before the primary.

ILEANA ROS-LEHTINEN

(Office of Representative Ros Lehtinen)

United States Representative
Republican of Florida
One Hundred First Congress
August 29, 1989–present

Ileana Ros-Lehtinen's victory in the special election of August 29, 1989, captured for Republicans a seat long held by Democratic Representative Claude Pepper. Ros-Lehtinen, who was born in Havana and represents a large Cuban-American population in Florida's Eighteenth District, also became the first Cuban-American elected to Congress.

Ros-Lehtinen was born July 15, 1952, and emigrated to the United States thirty years ago. She attended Miami-Dade Community College where she received an A.A. in 1972. She subsequently earned a B.A. in 1975 and a M.S. in 1987 from Florida International University. She is a candidate for a doctorate in education at the University of Miami. Ros-

Lehtinen taught school and was the founder and administrator of a private elementary school.

Beginning in 1982, Ros-Lehtinen served four years in the Florida House of Representatives and from 1986 to 1989 was a member of the state senate. She played a large role in the passage of legislation dealing with victims' rights, drug-free workplaces, and tuition assistance programs for Florida college students. Following the death of Claude Pepper in May 1989, Ros-Lehtinen entered the special election in which she defeated ten opponents. After taking the oath of office on September 6, 1989, she was assigned to the Committee on Foreign Affairs and the Committee on Government Operations.

MARGARET S. ROUKEMA

(Office of Representative Roukema)

United States Representative
Republican of New Jersey
Ninety-seventh–One Hundred First Congresses
January 3, 1981–present

Marge Roukema won election to the House of Representatives in 1980 when she defeated incumbent Representative Andrew Maguire in New Jersey's Seventh District. Two years later she was reelected from the newly-drawn Fifth District that encompasses the northern tier of the state from the suburbs near New York to the rural communities along the

Delaware River. Roukema was born Margaret Scafati in Newark, New Jersey, on September 19, 1929, and grew up in West Orange, New Jersey. She received her B.A. degree from Montclair State College in 1951 and subsequently pursued graduate studies there. In 1975 she undertook graduate work in city and regional planning at Rutgers University.

Roukema taught school in the 1950s and was later involved in various community affairs. She entered public life as a member of the Ridgewood (N.J.) Board of Education from 1970 to 1973. Also active in local party politics, Roukema served as president of the Ridgewood Republican Club in 1977 and 1978 and made her first run against Maguire as Republican nominee for the House in 1978.

After her successful campaign of 1980, Roukema gained seats on the Committee on Education and Labor and the Committee on Banking, Finance and Urban Affairs where she has continued to serve throughout her term. In the Ninety-eighth Congress she joined the newly-formed Select Committee on Hunger. From her committee assignments, Roukema has pursued such legislative interests as job training in the private sector, child support, welfare reform and family leave policy.

PATRICIA FUKUDA SAIKI

(Office of Representative Saiki)

United States Representative
Republican of Hawaii
One Hundredth–One Hundred First Congresses
January 3, 1987–present

Upon her election to the House of Representatives in 1986, Patricia Saiki brought with her extensive experience in the Republican Party organization of Hawaii and in the state legislature. After working as a junior and senior high school teacher, she entered politics as a delegate to the state Constitutional Convention in 1968 and also was elected to the Hawaii House of Representatives that year. She served in that body until 1974 and was a member of the state senate from 1974 to 1983. Saiki was the Republican nominee for lieutenant governor in 1982 and from 1983 to 1985 served as chair of the Republican Party of Hawaii.

Saiki was born Patricia Fukuda in Hilo, Hawaii, on May 28, 1930, and attended public schools in her native city before graduating with a B.S. from the University of Hawaii at Manoa in 1952. As a resident of Honolulu in September 1986, she entered the special election to fill the vacancy left in Hawaii's First District when Cecil Heftel resigned the seat to run for governor. Saiki lost the special election to Neil Abercrombie but won the Republican primary, held on the same day, for the Republican nomination for the general election. By defeating Democratic candidate Mufi Hannemann in November, Saiki became the first Republican to represent Hawaii in the House since statehood.

In her two terms as a House Member, Saiki has served on the Committee on Banking, Finance and Urban Affairs, the Committee on Merchant Marine and Fisheries, and the Select Committee on Aging. She was a cosponsor of the bill to provide compensation for Japanese-Americans interned during the Second World War and she helped secure authorization for the inclusion of new land in the Kiluea National Wildlife Refuge. In September 1990, Saiki won the Republican nomination for the U.S. Senate.

KATHARINE PRICE COLLIER ST. GEORGE

United States Representative
Republican of New York
Eightieth–Eighty-eighth Congresses
January 3, 1947–January 3, 1965

A life-time resident of one of the first American communities founded as a haven for millionaires and the home of the men's dinner jacket, Katharine St. George was also a first cousin of Franklin D. Roosevelt. She was born Katharine Delano Price Collier on July 12, 1894, in Bridgnorth, England, where her father was serving as European editor of *Forum* magazine. At the age of two she came to the United States with her parents and resided in Tuxedo, New York. Nine years later she returned to Europe and was educated in England, France, Switzerland and Germany. Following her father's death in 1913 she returned to Tuxedo and married George St. George in April 1917. Katharine St. George served as executive vice president and treasurer of her husband's coal brokerage firm, a member of the Tuxedo town board from 1926 to 1949, and a member of the Tuxedo board of education from 1926 to 1946.

With Franklin Roosevelt's election as president in 1932, St. George ceased campaigning for her fellow Republicans, but reentered politics in 1940 to oppose a third term for her cousin. In 1942 she lost her bid for Republican nomination to the state assembly, but she chaired the Orange County campaign committee and worked for the reelection of Twenty-ninth District Representative Hamilton Fish and others.

In 1944 Hamilton Fish lost his seat to Augustus W. Bennet, a Republican who had lost to Fish in the primary and then ran on the Democratic and American Labor Party ticket in the general election. When Bennet sought the regular Republican nomination in 1946, St. George defeated him in the August primary with help of Fish and local unions angered by Bennet's votes on labor issues. She went on to defeat Democrat James K. Welsh in the general election.

St. George served on the Committee on Post Office and Civil Service, the Committee on Government Operations, the Committee on Armed Services, and the Rules Committee. Attentive to the needs of her milk and poultry producing district, she submitted bills in 1954 to authorize the Defense Department to use surplus butter in the rations provided to the armed forces and to limit reductions in dairy price supports. In June 1959 she suggested establishment of marketing regulations to stabilize the broiler and egg industry.

During her first term, St. George proposed legislation to expand the provisions of the Veterans' Administration law to cover Women's Army Auxiliary Corps personnel. Although she failed in 1950 to obtain Judici-

ary Committee approval to report to the full House a proposed Equal Rights Amendment for women, her 1959 proposal to outlaw sex discrimination in payment of wages became law in the form of the Equal Pay Act of 1963.

In the midst of a January 1950 work slowdown by soft coal miners, St. George offered a concurrent resolution asking President Truman to invoke the national emergency provisos of the Taft-Hartley Act. In May 1953 she proposed legislation to grant the Postmaster General, rather than Congress, authority to increase postal rates. During the 1950s she submitted bills to establish a federal safety division in the Labor Department, supply a code of ethics for government service, and to prohibit payment of Veterans' Administration gratuities to anyone belonging to an organization which advocated the overthrow of the United States government.

In July 1961 St. George joined seven other Rules Committee members in voting to table the Kennedy administration's proposal to furnish states with funding for school construction and teacher salaries. Four days after the Supreme Court's June 1962 decision prohibiting the use of an official prayer in New York state schools, she introduced a joint resolution authorizing Congress to override Supreme Court decisions by two-thirds majority vote of both houses. Along with Representative H.R. Gross of Iowa, she dissented from the Post Office and Civil Service Committee's favorable report on a 1963 bill to increase the salaries of federal career employees, including Members of Congress, and voted against the measure when it was passed by the House in June 1964.

St. George sought a tenth term in 1964 but was defeated by John G. Dow. She chaired Tuxedo Park's Republican town committee until 1979 and was a resident until her death there on May 2, 1983.

CLAUDINE SCHNEIDER

(Office of Representative Schneider)

United States Representative
Republican of Rhode Island
Ninety-seventh–One Hundred First Congresses
January 3, 1981–present

For five terms, Claudine Schneider has won election as a Republican in a traditionally Democratic district while continuing to speak out on a wide variety of national issues. She first ran for Congress in 1978 when she unsuccessfully challenged incumbent Democrat Edward Beard. Two years later she won the seat in a repeat contest and became the first Republican from Rhode Island to serve in the House in more than forty years. Schneider was born Claudine Cmarada in Clairton, Pennsylvania, on March 25, 1947. She attended the University of Barcelona in Spain and Rosemont College in Pennsylvania before receiving her B.A. from Windham College in Vermont in 1969. She later attended the University of Rhode Island School of Community Planning. In the 1970s, Schneider became involved in a number of environmental concerns, serving as founder of the Rhode Island Committee on Energy in 1973, executive director of the Conservation Law Foundation in 1974 and federal coordinator of Rhode Island Coastal Management Program in 1978. Before election to Congress, she worked as a television producer and talk-show host.

Since her first term in Congress, Schneider has served on the Committee on Merchant Marine and Fisheries and the Committee on Science, Space and Technology. In the Ninety-eighth Congress she joined the Select Committee on Aging. In Congress, Schneider has continued to focus on environmental issues. She played a central role in the decision to halt construction of the Clinch River nuclear reactor. She helped lead the effort to ban ocean dumping of sludge and medical waste. In addition to her role in shaping environmental policy, Schneider helped gain passage of the Civil Rights Restoration Act in 1988. After five terms in Congress, Schneider has announced that she will run for the U.S. Senate seat held by Claiborne Pell rather than seek reelection to the House in 1990.

PATRICIA S. SCHROEDER

(Office of Representative Schroeder)

United States Representative
Democrat of Colorado
Ninety-third–One Hundred First Congresses
January 3, 1973–present

In her nine terms in Congress, Pat Schroeder has concentrated her legislative efforts on issues ranging from arms control to welfare reform to benefits for federal workers. First elected to the House on an anti-Vietnam War platform in 1972, she quickly won a seat on the Armed Services Committee where she remains a leading advocate of arms control, responsible defense spending and improved benefits and working conditions for military personnel. As the longest-serving woman in the One Hundred First Congress, she also has earned national recognition as a proponent of women's and family issues. Among her achievements have been the Family and Medical Leave Act and a block grant to fund day-care centers for school-age children.

Schroeder was born Patricia Scott in Portland, Oregon, on July 30, 1940, and was raised in Texas, Ohio, and Iowa. She graduated from the University of Minnesota with a B.A. in 1961 and received her J.D. from Harvard Law School in 1964. She began her law practice in Colorado as a field attorney with the National Labor Relations Board for two years and later entered private practice. Schroeder also taught law at Denver area schools.

In 1972 Schroeder entered her first political contest when she sought the Democratic nomination to challenge incumbent Representative James McKevitt for Colorado's First District seat in the House of Representatives.

After securing the party nomination, Schroeder won a close election in what has since been a safe district for her. In addition to her appointment to the Armed Services Committee in her first term, she served on the Committee on Post Office and Civil Service where she was chair of the Subcommittee on Civil Service from the Ninety-sixth through One Hundredth Congresses. In the One Hundred First Congress she became chair of the Armed Services Subcommittee on Military Installations. Since the Ninety-seventh Congress Schroeder has been a member of the Committee on the Judiciary as well. She is also a member of the Select Committee on Children, Youth and Families. Schroeder serves as co-chair of the Congressional Caucus for Women's Issues, which she helped to found.

EDNA OAKES SIMPSON

United States Representative
Republican of Illinois
Eighty-sixth Congress
January 3, 1959–January 3, 1961

Edna Simpson stood for election to the House from Illinois' Twentieth District in November 1988, just nine days after the death of her husband, eight-term Representative Sidney Simpson. The district's Republican committee selected Edna Simpson to take her husbands' place on the ballot for the office to which he had been renominated. Although

she did not make any campaign appearances, Edna Simpson easily defeated Quincy attorney Henry W. Pollock for the seat in the Eighty-sixth Congress.

She served on the Committee on House Administration and the Committee on Interior and Insular Affairs. Although the reclusive Simpson never spoke on the floor, she did propose an amendment to the Railroad Retirement Act that retirees who received veterans' benefits would also receive their full annuities. In December of 1959, she announced that she would not seek a second term in Congress.

Edna Simpson was born in Carrollton, Illinois, on October 26, 1891. She died in Alton, Illinois, on May 15, 1984.

LOUISE M. SLAUGHTER

(Office of Representative Slaughter)

United States Representative
Democrat of New York
One Hundred–One Hundred First Congresses
January 3, 1987–present

A native of Harlan County, Kentucky, Louise Slaughter has spent most of her adult life in upstate New York where she has represented metropolitan Rochester and its surrounding counties since 1987. Entering politics in the early 1970s as a proponent of local environmental issues, Slaughter defeated incumbents to win seats in the Monroe County legislature in 1975 and the New York Assembly in 1983. Between elective posts, from 1979 to 1982, Slaughter directed then Lieutenant Governor Mario Cuomo's regional office in Rochester. In challenging one-term Republican Representative Fred Eckert in New York's Thirtieth District in 1986, Slaughter became one of five candidates and the only woman to defeat a sitting member of Congress that year.

After two-and-one-half years in Congress, Slaughter was appointed to the powerful House Rules Committee in June 1989 to fill the vacancy left by the death of committee chairman Claude Pepper. Slaughter resigned from the Committee on Government Operations and Committee on Public Works and Transportation to take the new post. She continues as a member of the Select Committee on Aging where she has authored legislation to protect senior citizens from insurance fraud and to fund a preventive-medicine program for the elderly. More recently Slaughter has written legislation to ensure that homeless children can attend public school and to create a national commission to improve federal support of local law enforcement agencies.

Slaughter was born Louise McIntosh on August 14, 1929. She attended the University of Kentucky where she received a B.S. in 1951 and a master's degree in public health in 1953.

MARGARET CHASE SMITH

(U.S. Senate Historical Office)

Republican of Maine
United States Representative
Seventy-sixth–Eightieth Congresses
June 3, 1940–January 3, 1949
United States Senator
January 3, 1949–January 3, 1973

In more than three decades of service in both houses of Congress, Margaret Chase Smith earned a reputation for personal independence and integrity. She was born Margaret Madeline Chase in Skowhegan, Maine, on December 14, 1897. She graduated from Sko-

whegan High School in 1916 and was a primary school teacher for two years. Beginning in 1919, she worked as a telephone operator and commercial manager of a telephone company, circulation manager of a weekly newspaper, office manager of a woolen mills, and treasurer of a waste process company.

In May 1930 she married Skowhegan businessman and newspaper owner Clyde H. Smith. At the same time she began her political career as a member of the Republican state committee, serving until her husband's election to the House from Maine's Second District six years later.

Clyde Smith died on April 8, 1940, one day after he withdrew as a candidate for reelection due to ill health. Margaret Chase Smith, whom he had urged to run in his place, was elected to fill the vacancy on June 3. She soon demonstrated her independence from the Republican leadership when she broke with a majority of her colleagues to vote for the Lend-Lease agreement with Britain and for the Selective Training and Service Act. At the beginning of the Seventy-eighth Congress in 1943 she was appointed to the Naval Affairs Committee and in that capacity took part in an investigation of the construction of destroyers and inspected bases in the South Pacific. Smith was particularly interested in securing permanent regular status for women who served in auxiliary units in the armed forces and worked for passage of the 1948 Women's Armed Services Integration Act. She also favored the 1947 armed forces unification bill.

In domestic affairs, particularly in the areas of Social Security and labor legislation, Smith supported the policies of Presidents Truman and Roosevelt more often than most Republicans. She opposed the 1946 Case strike-control bill and voted against legislation to change the Committee on Un-American Activities from a special to a standing committee of the House. In addition to her assignment on Naval Affairs, Smith served on numerous House committees including Elections, War Claims, Revision of the Laws, Invalid Pensions, Education, Post Office and Post Roads, and Armed Services.

When Maine's senior United States senator, majority leader Wallace White, announced in August 1947 that he would not seek a fourth term in 1948, Smith entered the race to succeed him and was easily elected after defeat-ing Governor Horace A. Hildreth and former Governor Sumner Sewall in a hotly-contested primary race. She was reelected to the Senate three times. From June 1, 1955, until September 6, 1968 (when she was recovering from hip surgery) she answered the Senate roll call for 2,941 consecutive votes. Initially appointed to the Senate Committee on the District of Columbia and the Committee on Expenditures in Executive Departments, Smith also served on Rules and Administration, Appropriations, Armed Services, Government Operations, and Aeronautical and Space Sciences.

In a June 1, 1950, Senate speech entitled "A Declaration of Conscience," Smith attacked Wisconsin's Senator Joseph R. McCarthy (without referring to him by name) for using congressional immunity to make unproven charges that defamed innocent Americans and accused him of dividing the nation with his tactics. Although the speech attracted favorable nationwide attention and was endorsed by six fellow Republicans in the Senate, it did little to restrain McCarthy and his supporters. In the June 1954 primary, Smith won over 82 percent of the vote over Robert L. Jones, who was endorsed by McCarthy, and she was among the senators who voted to censure McCarthy in December of the same year.

In 1956 Smith proposed legislation which called for the enlargement of the research and training capacity of the National Institutes of Health, assistance to medical schools and a medical research facility construction plan. In September 1961 she criticized President Kennedy for failing to convince the Soviet Union that he possessed the resolution and fortitude to utilize the nation's nuclear capability, and she voted against the 1963 Test Ban Treaty. During the 1960s Smith's crusade to have the rose designated the official flower of the United States evoked much public comment, but her campaign was unable to overcome Senate Republican leader Everett M. Dirksen's decided preference for the marigold. (Legislation naming the rose the official flower was signed into law in October 1987).

On January 27, 1964, Smith declared her candidacy for the Republican presidential nomination and received primary votes in New Hampshire, Illinois, Massachusetts, Texas, Oregon among others and twenty-seven first ballot votes at the Republican national convention.

On June 1, 1970, the twentieth anniversary of her original "Declaration of Conscience," Smith spoke out once more, criticizing the extremist tactics employed by student militants as well as the attempts of the Nixon administration to repress dissent and polarize the nation. She strayed from party orthodoxy by opposing the supersonic transport plane, the "Safeguard" anti-ballistic missile system, and the nominations of Clement F. Haynsworth, Jr., and G. Harrold Carswell to the Supreme Court.

To the surprise of many across the country, the venerable woman from Maine was rejected by the Maine voters in her bid for a fifth term in 1972. Before the election, Smith gave serious thought to retirement but decided to run to rebut charges that she was too old at seventy-four to continue to serve effectively. The Democratic nominee, Second District Representative William D. Hathaway, emphasized Smith's age and charged that she was ineffective in Washington and inaccessible at home. Her failure to maintain an office in Maine was cited as evidence that she was out of touch with the state's concerns.

In retirement from public office Smith has devoted much of her attention to the affairs of the Margaret Chase Smith Library Center at the Northwood Institute in Skowhegan, where she still resides.

VIRGINIA DODD SMITH

United States Representative
Republican of Nebraska
Ninety-fourth–One Hundred First Congresses
January 3, 1975–present

Throughout her congressional term, Virginia Smith has concentrated on the same agricultural issues at the center of her earlier career. As the wife of a Nebraska wheat farmer, Smith became involved in a wide variety of farm organizations such as the American Farm Bureau Federation, of which she was chair of the women's bureau from 1955 to 1974, the United States Department of Agriculture's Home Economics Research Advisory Committee and the American Country Life Association. In addition to serving on various government commissions before entering Congress, Smith was active in the state Republican Party and delegate to the party's national conventions from 1956 to 1972.

Smith was born Virginia Dodd in Randolph, Iowa, on June 30, 1911, and was raised in that state. In 1936 she received her B.A. in education from the University of Nebraska. Smith's extensive participation in farming organizations and civic affairs in Nebraska provided a base for her first bid for elective office when she ran for the House seat in Nebraska's Third District in 1974. After narrowly defeating the Democratic candidate in her initial campaign, Smith has easily won reelection in the seven succeeding campaigns.

As a freshman in Congress, Smith served on the Committee on Education and Labor and the Committee on Interior and Insular Affairs. In her second term she left those committees and gained a seat on the Committee on Appropriations where she continues to serve. She is the ranking Republican member of the Subcommittee on Rural Development, Agriculture and Related Agencies. Smith has consistently worked to protect the interests of the many grain farmers and cattle ranchers who populate her district.

Smith announced in 1989 that she would not be a candidate for reelection in 1990.

OLYMPIA JEAN SNOWE

(Office of Representative Snowe)

United States Representative
Republican of Maine
Ninety-sixth–One Hundred First Congresses
January 3, 1979–present

In 1978 Olympia Snowe was elected to the House seat previously held by William Cohen for whom she had worked as a district staff assistant. Snowe's varied experience in Maine politics helped secure her unanimous nomination as the Republican candidate for the Second District representative. She defeated the Democratic candidate in the general election and has easily won reelection since.

Snowe was born Olympia Jean Bouchles on February 21, 1947, in Augusta, Maine, to Greek immigrant parents. She grew up in Auburn, Maine, and graduated from the University of Maine in 1969. Following the death of her husband in 1973, Snowe was elected to fill his seat in the Maine House of Representatives. She also directed her late husband's concrete company. In 1977 Snowe moved on to the state senate where she served until entering Congress in 1979.

In her first House term, Snowe served on the Committee on Government Operations and the Committee on Small Business. In the Ninety-seventh Congress she left the former for a seat on the Committee on Foreign Affairs where she continues to serve and is the ranking Republican on the Subcommittee on International Operations. As a member of this subcommittee she was part of the team that inspected the new U.S. embassy in Moscow and recommended that it be rebuilt to eliminate Soviet listening devices. Snowe also has served on the Select Committee on Aging since the Ninety-sixth Congress and the Joint Economic Committee since the Ninety-eighth Congress.

In addition to her committee work, Snowe serves as co-chair of the Congressional Caucus on Women's Issues and was a co-founder of the '92 Group of Republican representatives seeking to gain a majority for that party in the House of Representatives.

GLADYS NOON SPELLMAN

(U.S. House of Representatives)

United States Representative
Democrat of Maryland
Ninety-fourth–Ninety-seventh Congresses
January 3, 1975–February 24, 1981

A tireless supporter of federal employees, Gladys Spellman was born Gladys Blossom Noon in New York City on March 1, 1918, and attended public schools in New York City and Washington, D.C. After attending George Washington University and the graduate school of the United States Department of Ag-

riculture, she taught in the public schools of Prince Georges County, Maryland.

Spellman was elected a member of the Prince Georges County Board of Commissioners in 1962 and was reelected in 1966. During her second term she was council chair for two years. From 1971 to 1974 she served as councilwoman at-large. In 1974 she easily won the

Democratic nomination in a September primary for the Fifth District seat in the House of Representatives being vacated by Lawrence J. Hogan and defeated Republican John B. Burcham, Jr., in the general election.

During her three terms in Congress, Spellman served on the Committee on Banking, Currency and Housing (renamed the Banking, Finance and Urban Affairs Committee after the Ninety-fourth Congress), the Committee on Post Office and Civil Service, and the Democratic Steering and Policy Committee. In 1977 she favored legislation to establish a bank to make loans to cooperatives owned by consumers and legislation to extend the federal revenue-sharing program. She also voted for a 1975 proposal authorizing $7 billion in loan guarantees for financially troubled New York City.

Spellman frequently used her position as chair of the Post Office and Civil Service Committee's Subcommittee on Compensation and Employee Benefits to advance the interests of federal employees. She resisted restrictions on the hiring or promotion of federal workers and opposed President Carter's plan to reform the civil service system in 1978. She was particularly critical of the proposed Senior Executive Service, which she feared would politicize the civil service. She favored an amendment to the Intergovernmental Personnel Act of 1970 which would have authorized a subsidy to train civil servants in labor-management relations. She also supported adjusted cost-of-living increases in the pay of military retirees and a measure requiring federal employees to inform spouses if they elected not to provide survivors' benefits payments.

On October 31, 1980, Spellman was stricken with a heart attack while campaigning for a fourth term. Although she overwhelmed Republican Kevin R. Igoe at the polls four days later, she remained in a semiconscious state, and on February 24, 1981, her seat was declared vacant by the House since she was unable to discharge the duties of her office. Her husband Reuben was a Democratic candidate in the April special primary to choose nominees to succeed her but finished second in a field of six candidates. Gladys Spellman died in Rockville, Maryland, on June 19, 1988.

WINNIFRED CLAIRE STANLEY

(U.S. House of Representatives)

United States Representative
Republican of New York
Seventy-eighth Congress
January 3, 1943–January 3, 1945

Winnifred Stanley interrupted her distinguished legal career only briefly to serve a single term in the House of Representatives. She agreed to be a candidate for an at-large seat that all expected to be eliminated in the ensuing redistricting plan drawn in accordance with New York's loss of two House seats following the census of 1940. During her service in the wartime Congress, she worked to facilitate the return to peace and to reduce the influence of the federal government once the military emergency passed.

Stanley was born in the Bronx, New York, on August 14, 1909, and moved as a young girl to Buffalo. She graduated from the University of Buffalo in 1930 and received a law degree from the same university in 1933. After four years in private law practice, Stanley was appointed assistant district attorney for Erie County in 1938. She specialized in the prosecution of cases dealing with women and children and served in that office until she ran for Congress.

In 1942 the Republican Party of New York recommended that the state's two at-large seats in Congress be eliminated, and they sought a candidate for the at-large election who would be willing to step down at the end of a single term. At the party convention in Saratoga Springs they nominated Winnifred Stanley who set off to campaign with gubernatorial candidate Thomas Dewey. In a campaign that emphasized the need to prepare for a stable peace, Stanley promised to make official Washington observe the same sacrifices that faced the rest of the nation and to seek further protection against sabotage. In the November election she led a field of eight contenders for the two seats.

Eager to gain a seat on the Committee on the Judiciary once the Seventy-eighth Congress convened, the freshman Stanley settled for appointment to the Committee on Civil Service and the Committee on Patents. If her committee assignments were a disappointment, she nevertheless promoted favorite programs such as a proposed equal-pay-for-equal-work amendment to the National Labor Relations Act, though it failed to pass. Stanley generally voted in line with her fellow Republicans and opposed many of Roosevelt's programs to maintain New Deal programs for farm supports and soil conservation. She agreed with the Democratic administration in her vote to eliminate all poll taxes.

With the elimination of New York's at-large seats, Stanley was not a candidate for reelection in 1944. Governor Dewey appointed her chief counsel of the New York State Employees' Retirement System in January of 1945, and she served in that office for ten years. From 1955 to 1979 she was assistant attorney general with the New York State Law Department. She continued to practice law in Albany and then Kenmore, New York, until her retirement in 1986. She is a resident of Kenmore.

LEONOR KRETZER SULLIVAN

United States Representative
Democrat of Missouri
Eighty-third–Ninety-fourth Congresses
January 3, 1953–January 3, 1977

The only woman representative from Missouri, Leonor Sullivan was a defender of consumers and the author of the food stamp plan that distributed federally owned surplus food to the poor. She was born August 21, 1902, in St. Louis, Missouri, and attended public and private schools in that city. She also enrolled in night classes at Washington University, taught business arithmetic and accounting, and served as director of the St. Louis Comptometer School. In 1941 she married Eleventh District Representative John B. Sullivan and served as his campaign manager and administrative aide from 1942 until his death in January 1951. She then worked as a secretary to Missouri Congressman Theodore Irving until

May 1952, when she resigned to campaign for congressional nomination from the Third District. She was elected over Claude I. Bakewell who had succeeded to her husband's seat in the Eighty-second Congress.

In 1957 and 1959 Sullivan offered proposals to revive a surplus food stamp program that the Department of Agriculture had administered from 1939 to 1943, but she failed to win approval. In 1959 Congress ratified amendments proposed by her and Minnesota Senator Hubert Humphrey empowering the Agriculture Department to manage a food stamp plan, but the Department did not discharge the authority. Although an experimental program for selected depressed areas had been instituted by executive order in 1961, it was not until August 1964 that Congress passed and President Johnson signed a law sponsored by Sullivan establishing a permanent food stamp program.

Sullivan also sponsored legislation to protect consumers from hazardous substances, harmful food color additives and cosmetics, and tainted meat and poultry. She was the House floor manager for the 1968 Consumer Credit Protection Act which established "truth in lending" provisions requiring lenders to provide consumers with information about the cost of credit.

Sullivan served on the Committee on Banking and Currency, the Committee on Merchant Marine and Fisheries, and the Joint Committee on Defense Production. During the Ninety-third and Ninety-fourth Congresses (1973-1977) she chaired the Committee on Merchant Marine and Fisheries. Among her accomplishments was passage of the 1976 Fishery and Conservation Management Act, which established a two-hundred mile fisheries conservation zone off the coasts of the United States.

Sullivan declined to be a candidate for renomination in 1976 and was succeeded by Richard A. Gephardt. She was a resident of St. Louis until her death on September 1, 1988.

JESSIE SUMNER

United States Representative
Republican of Illinois
Seventy-sixth–Seventy-ninth Congresses
January 3, 1939–January 3, 1947

In the latter days of the New Deal and throughout the Second World War, Jessie Sumner maintained a determined opposition to the domestic and foreign policies of President Franklin Roosevelt. As one of the most extreme proponents of nonintervention and isolationism, Sumner found herself an increasingly lonely voice in the debate on the crucial issues of the 1940s.

Sumner was born in Milford, Illinois, on July 17, 1898. She graduated from Girton School in Winnetka, Illinois, in 1916 and Smith College in 1920. She studied law at the University of Chicago, Columbia University and Oxford University, and briefly enrolled at the University of Wisconsin at Madison and New York University School of Commerce. In 1923 she entered practice in Chicago and after working for Chase Manhattan Bank in New York in 1928 and 1929, she returned to Milford where she continued to practice law.

In her first electoral bid, Sumner lost the primary for state's attorney but she was elected judge of Iroquois County in 1937 to fill the unexpired term of her uncle. The following year she entered the race for a seat in the House of Representatives from Illinois' Eighteenth District. Running as an outspoken critic of the New Deal, Sumner defeated Democrat James A. Meeks.

Sumner served as a member of the Committee on Banking and Currency throughout her term in Congress, but she devoted most of her attention to issues of foreign policy and military preparedness. A fervent isolationist, Sumner opposed amending the Neutrality Act to permit the arming of American merchant ships carrying war materiel. After the outbreak of war in Europe, she castigated Roosevelt for conducting much of his foreign policy in secret and accused him of mismanaging funds allocated for national defense. She continued to criticize the war effort after American entry into hostilities and opposed any invasion of Western Europe that would relieve pressure on the Soviet Union by opening a second front against Nazi Germany. She declared in March 1944 that it made no difference whether Hitler or Stalin dominated Europe and warned that an invasion might cost a million lives. That spring Sumner offered an amendment to postpone D-Day.

One of Sumner's few legislative achievement during the Second World War came during consideration of a $20 billion naval appropriations bill in January 1942, when she secured an amendment that prohibited the use of parties, champagne or gifts during the launching of new ships. Such ceremonies she declared harmful to the morale of armed forces personnel, defense workers and overtaxed private citizens.

Sumner was a bitter opponent of Representative J. William Fulbright's 1943 resolution which endorsed United States participation in the establishment of international machinery to establish and maintain peace. Always suspicious of British as well as Soviet allies, Sumner accused Great Britain of trying to limit the authority of Army Chief of Staff George C. Marshall and General Douglas MacArthur. Her fear that the Soviet Union might use its supervisory power over relief operations to influence the policies of countries it had liberated from German occupation led her to oppose the establishment of the United Nations Relief and Rehabilitation Administration.

Sumner's fiscal conservatism and distrust of international commitments persisted in the postwar era. In June 1945 she criticized legislation authorizing United States entrance into the World Bank and the International Monetary Fund as the worst fraud in American history. In March 1946 she voted to terminate an emergency housing bill for veterans, sponsored by Representative Wright Patman of Texas and supported by the Truman administration.

Sumner declined to be a candidate for renomination in 1946 and returned to Milford to resume her position as vice president and later president of the Sumner National Bank. She is a resident of Milford.

LERA MILLARD THOMAS

United States Representative
Democrat of Texas
Eighty-ninth Congress
March 26, 1966–January 3, 1967

In serving out the remainder of her late husband's term, Lera Thomas attempted to further his support of the space program and other economic interests of their Houston, Texas, district. Albert Thomas, a twenty-nine year veteran of the House of Representatives, had been chairman of the Appropriations subcommittee on defense and helped win for Houston the Manned Spacecraft Center. Lera Thomas called on Congress to appropriate funds for the construction of NASA's lunar sample receiving laboratory in Houston. From her seat on the Committee on Merchant Marine and Fisheries, she also sought further funding of the Houston Ship Channel which had been another project of her husband.

On March 26, 1966, Lera Thomas won the special election held to fill the vacancy in the Eighth District created by her husband's death. Although she faced a Republican opponent, Louis Leman, he encouraged voters to elect Thomas. She won nearly three-quarters of the vote. Texas election law kept Albert Thomas's name on the ballot of the May 7 primary for the Democratic nomination to the Ninetieth Congress. A victory for the deceased Thomas would have permitted the Harris County Democratic Executive Committee to name Lera Thomas as the party's candidate in the fall election, but she discouraged the movement to gain her another term in office.

Lera Millard was born in Nacogdoches, Texas, on August 3, 1900. She attended Brenau College in Gainesville, Georgia, and the University of Alabama. After retirement from the House of Representatives, she returned to her hometown where she operated a family farm and an antique business and where she still resides.

RUTH THOMPSON

United States Representative
Republican of Michigan
Eighty-second–Eighty-fourth Congresses
January 3, 1951–January 3, 1957

Ruth Thompson's background as a county probate judge and attorney with civilian and military government agencies prepared her to accept appointment as the first woman to sit on the House Judiciary Committee. She was born in Whitehall, Michigan, on September 15, 1887, attended public schools and graduated from Muskegon Business College in 1905.

Beginning in 1918 she worked in a law office and studied law in night school for six years before she was admitted to the bar. Thompson was also Registrar of the Probate Court of Muskegon County for eighteen years.

Thompson was elected Judge of Probate in Muskegon County and served from 1925 until 1937. After serving a term in the Michigan

House of Representatives from 1939 to 1941 she worked with the Social Security Board's Old-Age and Survivor's Insurance Division and the Labor Department's Wage and Hour Division. She spent the war years in the civilian personnel section of the Adjutant General's office. Following the end of hostilities in Europe she served the Adjutant General's bureau at Headquarters Command in Frankfurt, Germany, and Copenhagen, Denmark, returning to Michigan in 1946 to engage in the private practice of law.

In 1950 Ninth District Representative Albert J. Engel declined to run for a ninth term in order to seek the Republican nomination for governor. Thompson entered the race to fill his seat and was elected over the Democratic nominee, Noel P. Fox.

In addition to her seat on the Judiciary Committee, Thompson served on the Joint Committee on Immigration and Nationality Policy. A proponent of limited federal spending, she opposed much of the Truman administration's domestic program and joined conservative Republicans in calling for the removal of Secretary of State Acheson and occa-sionally voting against military and economic assistance for Western Europe.

Thompson sponsored proposals to encourage development of public library services in rural areas and stimulate the growth of low-cost electric energy from a variety of power sources. She introduced legislation to institute a Department of Peace, establish an academy for House page boys, and to make it easier for World War I veterans with honorable discharges to claim benefits.

Thompson's congressional career began to unravel when the Air Force announced that it planned to build a new jet interceptor base outside her district, despite her private and public protests that Air Force officials had promised her repeatedly that the base would be located inside the Ninth. Although she succeeded in reversing this decision, the resulting delay and additional construction costs brought local resentment to a fever pitch and led to her ouster by Robert P. Griffin in the August 1956 primary. Thompson returned to Whitehall and in 1965 became a patient at the Plainwell Sanitarium in Allegan County, where she died on April 5, 1970.

JOLENE UNSOELD

(Office of Representative Unsoeld)

United States Representative
Democrat of Washington
One Hundred First Congress
January 3, 1989–present

Jolene Unsoeld's first became involved in politics as a lobbyist in Washington's state capital, Olympia, where she worked for campaign finance reform and on various environmental issues in the 1970s and early 1980s. She was also a member of the Democratic National Committee from 1983 to 1988. In 1984 she was elected to the Washington House of

Representatives and served until she entered Congress in 1989.

A native of the Northwest, Unsoeld was born Jolene Bishoprick in Corvallis, Oregon, on December 3, 1931. She grew up in Oregon and Washington and spent several years of her childhood in Shanghai, China. She attended Oregon State University. With her husband, a mountain climber and educator, she lived in Kathmandu, Nepal, from 1962 to 1967. During that time she spent two years as director of the English Language Institute in Kathmandu.

As a member of the state legislature, Unsoeld gained attention for her work on environmental issues, including her successful campaign for a ballot initiative to establish more stringent requirements for the clean up of toxic-waste sites. Popular support for her efforts helped gain her the Democratic nomination for Congress from Washington's Third District. She narrowly defeated her Republican opponent in the general election. In her freshman term in Congress Unsoeld was appointed to the Committee on Merchant Marine and Fisheries, the Committee on Education and Labor and the Select Committee on Aging.

BARBARA F. VUCANOVICH

(Office of Representative Vucanovich)

United States Representative
Republican of Nevada
Ninety-eighth–One Hundred First Congresses
January 3, 1983–present

Although she never held office before her election to Congress, Barbara Vucanovich was active in Republican politics in Nevada for nearly thirty years as a delegate to state conventions and as a campaign worker in presidential elections. For twenty years she worked for Senator Paul Laxalt as a local organizer and later as his northern Nevada rep-

resentative. Her experience in party politics helped secure her the Republican nomination for the newly-created Second District seat in 1982. The Reno resident has since represented the district which encompasses most of the land area of Nevada.

Born Barbara Farrell at Camp Dix, N.J., on June 22, 1921, Vucanovich grew up in Albany,

N.Y., and attended Manhattanville College. She moved to Nevada in 1949 and entered business in the 1960s as the owner of an Evelyn Woods Reading Dynamics school and a travel agency.

As a Member of the House of Representatives, Vucanovich has centered on a variety of issues important to Nevada, including federal wilderness and national park policy, public land use and nuclear waste disposal. She serves on the Committee on Interior and Insular Affairs where she is ranking Republican on the Subcommittee on General Oversight and Investigations and on the Committee on House Administration where she is ranking Republican on the Subcommittee on Accounts. She is also a member of the Select Committee on Children, Youth and Families.

JESSICA McCULLOUGH WEIS

(U.S. House of Representatives)

United States Representative
Republican of New York
Eighty-sixth–Eighty-seventh Congresses
January 3, 1959–January 3, 1963

The daughter of a steel company executive, Jessica McCullough was born in Chicago on July 8, 1901, and soon moved with her family to Buffalo. She attended the Franklin School in Buffalo, Miss Wright's school in Bryn Mawr, Pennsylvania, and graduated from Madam Rieffel's School in New York City in 1917. In September 1921 she married Charles W. Weis, Jr., and moved to Rochester, New York, where she became active in the Junior League and charitable organizations.

Jessica, better known as "Judy," Weis' political career began in 1935, when Monroe County Republican leader Thomas E. Broderick named her vice chair of the Citizens' Republican Finance Committee. The following year she arranged motorcades for Republican presidential nominee Alfred M. Landon. In 1937 she became vice chair of the Monroe County Republican Committee, a post she held until 1952. Weis was president of the National Federation of Republican Women in 1941 and 1942. In 1943 she replaced former Representative Ruth Baker Pratt on the Republican National Committee and served there for the next two decades, attending many national party conventions. She was among the speakers who seconded the nomination of Thomas E. Dewey at the Republican National Convention of 1948 and was his associate campaign manager during the fall campaign.

In 1954 Weis was appointed an advisor to the United States delegate to the Inter-American Commission on Women. In 1953 President Eisenhower appointed her a member of the National Defense Civil Advisory Council. She was reappointed in 1956 and 1960.

With almost twenty years' experience in local and national party politics, Weis decided to run for elective office in 1958 and defeated Alphonse L. Cassetti for the House of Representatives seat from New York's Thirty-eighth District. She succeeded Kenneth B.

Keating, who was elected United States senator. In the Eighty-sixth Congress she served on the Committee on Government Operations and the Committee on the District of Columbia. In the succeeding Congress she left Government Operations to serve on the Committee on Science and Astronautics.

In committee and on the floor, Weis was generally a solid supporter of the Eisenhower administration. An advocate of economy in government, she opposed domestic spending initiatives for veterans' housing, airport and power plant construction and water pollution control. Weis supported a proposed Equal Rights Amendment to the Constitution, urged an end to wage discrimination against women, and supported the 1959 Landrum-Griffin Act designed to control illegal practices by labor unions.

In 1960, when Weis stood for reelection, she also coordinated the Republican congressional campaign in New York state. In June 1962 Weis informed the Republican State Committee that considerations of health prevented her from running for a third term. She was succeeded by Charles E. Goodell, who would later serve in the United States Senate. She died in Rochester on May 1, 1963.

EFFIEGENE LOCKE WINGO

United States Representative
Democrat of Arkansas
Seventy-first–Seventy-second Congress
November 4, 1930–March 3, 1933

Effiegene Wingo succeeded to her husband's seat in the House of Representatives at a time when her Arkansas district suffered the worst effects of the Depression as well as a series of natural disasters that devastated the agricultural economy. Although the problems facing the Fourth District were beyond the reach of any individual officeholder, Wingo arrived in office with an enviable range of support. Following the death of Otis Theodore Wingo in October 1930, both the Democratic and Republican central committees in the district nominated Effiegene Wingo for election to the unexpired term of her husband and to the Seventy-second Congress to which he had already won nomination. On November 4, 1930, she won the special election to the Seventy-first Congress and the general election to the succeeding term.

Wingo was sworn in on December 1, 1930, and served on the Committee on Accounts and the Committee on Insular Affairs. In the following Congress she served on the Committee on Foreign Affairs. She submitted legislation to establish a game refuge in the Ouachita National Forest and to create an Ouachita National Park. She sponsored a bill to complete construction of a railroad bridge across the Little River near Morris Ferry, Arkansas. She also sought various relief measures for her district. In February 1932 Wingo announced that she would not be a candidate for reelection.

Effiegene Locke, a great-great-great-granddaughter of Representative Matthew Locke of North Carolina, was born in Lockesburg, Arkansas on April 13, 1883. She studied music at the Union Female College in Oxford, Mississippi, and graduated from Maddox Seminary in Little Rock, Arkansas, in 1901. Her husband, whom she met at a Confederate veterans' reunion in DeQueen, Arkansas, was first elected to Congress in 1912. During the final four years of Otis Wingo's service in the House, Effiegene worked in his congressional office while he recuperated from an automobile accident.

Following her retirement from the House of Representatives, Effiegene Wingo was a cofounder of the National Institute of Public Affairs which provided students with internships in Washington. She later resided in DeQueen, Arkansas, until her death on a visit to Burlington, Ontario, on September 19, 1962.

CHASE GOING WOODHOUSE

United States Representative
Democrat of Connecticut
Seventy-ninth and Eighty-first Congresses
January 3, 1945–January 3, 1947
January 3, 1949–January 3, 1951

Throughout her lengthy and accomplished career, Chase Woodhouse moved easily between the worlds of public service and academics. In addition to her two terms in the House of Representatives, she served as an economic adviser and elected official in various governmental positions in between her several appointments as a college professor. In her congressional career she attempted to implement the same kind of economic policies that she recommended as a governmental adviser.

Margaret Chase Going was born in Victoria, British Columbia, on March 3, 1890. She grew up throughout the United States, attending schools in California, South Dakota, and Kentucky. In 1912 she graduated from McGill University in Montreal, Canada, and a year later received her M.A. from the same institution. She was briefly a social worker before going to Europe to study economics in Germany and England. She returned to become a fellow in political economy at the University of Chicago where she met and married a government professor, Edward Woodhouse, in 1917.

With her husband away in the armed services during the First World War, Chase Woodhouse accepted a teaching position at Smith College in Northampton, Massachusetts. In 1925 she left her job as an economics teacher to work as a senior economist for the home economics bureau of the Department of Agriculture. It was the beginning of a pattern that would persist through the remainder of her ninety-four years. She taught at the University of Texas, Teachers' College of Columbia University, and the University of Iowa and was director of personnel at the Women's College of the University of North Carolina before settling at the Connecticut College for Women from 1934 to 1946. In the meantime she was also a founder of the Institute of Women's Professional Relations and was chairman of research for the North Carolina Federation of Business and Professional Women's Clubs.

In Connecticut she continued her various professional commitments and in 1940 decided to add elective politics to her list of endeavors by running for secretary of state. She served one term during which she also served on the New London Town Committee and was chair of the Connecticut War Labor Board. In 1944, with the strong backing of organized labor,

Woodhouse was Democratic candidate for the House of Representatives from Connecticut's Second District and defeated one-term incumbent John McWilliams. As a freshman member of the House, Woodhouse was assigned to the Committee on Banking and Currency where she ardently worked for implementation of the Bretton Woods agreement to establish an international monetary fund and a world bank for redevelopment in the postwar era. She also fought for the maintenance of war-time price controls as a protection for consumers and for more affordable housing for returning veterans. In one of the controversial votes of the Seventy-ninth Congress, Woodhouse opposed making the Committee on Un-American Activities a standing committee.

Woodhouse failed in her bid for reelection in 1946 and accepted the position of executive director of the women's bureau of the Democratic National Committee from 1947 to 1948. In 1948 she served as an economic adviser to General Lucius Clay, the Allied military governor of Germany. That year she returned to Connecticut and regained her House seat from the Second District. She again served on the Committee on Banking and Currency and also on the Committee on House Administration, but she was unable to retain her seat in a reelection contest in 1950.

While her retirement from the House ended her career in elective office, Woodhouse continued in government as assistant to the director of Price Stabilization from 1951 to 1953. She was a delegate to the Connecticut Constitutional Convention in 1965. From 1952 to 1980, when she resigned at the age of ninety, she was director of the Service Bureau for Women's Organizations in Hartford, Connecticut. She was a resident of Sprague, Connecticut, until her death on December 12, 1984.